TABLE OF CONTENTS

ACRONYMS

AFG	Afghanistan
ARENA	*Alianza Republicana Nacionalista*
ARVN	Army of the Republic of Vietnam
CG	Civil Guard
CIA	Central Intelligence Agency
COIN	Counterinsurgency Operations
DIME	Diplomatic, Information, Military, Economic
DRA	Democratic Republic of Afghanistan
ERP	People's Revolutionary Army
ESAF	El Salvador Armed Forces
FDR	*Frente Democratico Revolucionario*
FID	Foriegn Internal Defense
FMLN	*Frente Farabundo Marti de Liberacion Nacional*
FPL	Popular Forces for Liberation
GOES	Government of El Salvador
GWOT	Global War on Terror
JIIM	Joint, Interagency, Intergovernmental, Multinational
MAAG	Military Advisory Assistance Group
MACV	Military Assistance Command—Vietnam
MILGRP	Military Group
NLF	National Liberation Front
OA	Operational Area
OCO	Overseas Contingency Operations
OEF	Operation Enduring Freedom
OEF-P	Operation Enduring Freedom—Philippines
OIF	Operation Iraqi Freedom

OPATT	Operations, Plans and Training Teams
ORDEN	*Organizacion Democratica Nacionalista*
OSS	Office of Strategic Services
PDC	*Partido Democrata Christiano*
RVN	Republic of Vietnam
SDC	Self Defense Corps
STABOPS	Stability Operations
USSR	Union of Socialist Soviet Republics
VC	Vietcong
WAS	Wide Area Security

ILLUSTRATIONS

INTRODUCTION

We see, therefore, that war is not merely an act of policy but a true political instrument, a continuation of political intercourse carried on with other means. [1]

— Carl von Clausewitz, 1827

All politics is local. [2]

— Speaker of the House Tip O'Neill, 1987

As the conflict in Afghanistan reaches its 13th and presumably final year of American involvement, military and academic writers have choked bookshelves with musings which lessons we Americans can garner from our longest conflict. Current regional assessments, socio-political analysis, and tactical-level battle histories may define some aspects of the Afghan conflict, but they lack the long-term assessment of the effect of a war on the relative security and stability of Afghanistan. Vietnam, concluded in 1975, and El Salvador, concluded in 1992, both offer such post-conflict assessment opportunities. In comparison to Afghanistan, volumes have been written by a myriad of sources about the Vietnam conflict, and the escalation of American interaction there from 1950-1973. Though still an authoritarian communist country ruled by the political elite, modern Vietnam has a booming economy that has brought international investors flocking to it, and created regional competition against local hegemonic power China for strategic resources. [3] El Salvador is presently 20-plus years post-conflict, and is demonstrating similar positive trends, such as increased domestic per capita income, lower infant mortality rates, and

---

[1]Carl von Clausewitz, *On War*, trans. by Michael Eliot Howard and Peter Paret (Princeton: Princeton University Press, 1989), 87.

[2]Tip O'Neill and William Novak, *Man of the House: The Life and Political Memoirs of Speaker Tip O'Neill* (New York: Random House, 1987), 43. Grammatical error in original copy.

[3]Freedom House, "Vietnam," Freedom in the World, http://www.freedomhouse.org/report/freedom-world/2013/vietnam#.U0rkuO9OXX4 (accessed 13 March 2014).

higher gross national product relative to its neighbors in Central America.[4] While each conflict cost both sets of belligerents untold blood and treasure, both countries are positive members of the global economic and social community.

Research Questions

There were a number of similarities, obviously differing in scale, between the American interaction in the conflict in Vietnam and in El Salvador, but multiple questions emerge. Why did the United States commit a force density that resulted in nearly 60,000 Americans killed in action, 111 billion dollars spent between 1965 and 1975, and 25 years committed to the Indochina Peninsula, and only a fraction of that commitment in the much more regionally volatile area in Central America?[5] Why did the initial American efforts in South Vietnam transition through a slowly evolving but nonetheless large-scale escalation and investment of American blood and treasure, which only ended in defeat and conquest by North Vietnam? How did El Salvador, despite a far smaller American intercession, not fall outright to the predations of the Communist-leaning *Frente Farabundo Marti de Liberacion Nacional* (FMLN)?[6]

Evidence presented in this monograph demonstrates that there is a relationship between the focus of advisorship effort at the appropriate echelons of a burgeoning counter-insurgent

---

[4]Freedom House, "El Salvador,"; Lujan Fernando, *Light Footprints: The Future of American Military Intervention*, Voices From the Field (Washington, DC: Center for a New American Security, 2013), 35, http://www.cnas.org/publications/reports/light-footprints-the-future-of-american-military-intervention#.U0mc9-9OXX4 (accessed 12 February 2014). Since the Civil War, El Salvador has sufficiently advanced as a secure nation, going as far as assisting the Allied efforts in Iraq with combat battalions.

[5]Andrew Krepinevich Jr., *The Army and Vietnam* (Baltimore: Johns Hopkins University Press, 1986), 23-25; Michael Lind, *Vietnam: The Necessary War: A Reinterpretation of America's Most Disastrous Military Conflict* (New York: Simon and Schuster, 1999), 256-58.

[6]Tommie Sue Montgomery, *Revolution in El Salvador: From Civil Strife to Civil Peace* (Boulder, CO: Westview Press, 1995), 5-6.

2

fight, and eventual mission success or failure. During the early stages of Vietnam, America focused on advisement and support activities with the Republic of South Vietnam tactical elements, which is opposite of the American involvement in the El Salvadoran Civil War, which focused mainly on diplomatic and economic efforts at the ministerial and policy levels, with marginal direct military support at echelons below brigade. A key ingredient in the recipe for success in the El Salvador conflict was the advisory effort placed on the liberal and transparent aspects of statehood and the mechanisms by which the government addressed the grievances of the populace. This focus serves as a lesson for future applications of American interventional power. Ignoring the levels of nepotism and corruption at the state and sub-state levels of governance and military leadership in Vietnam led to failure of America's advisor mission, and was a key ingredient in the eventual escalation of the war.

Like the early stages of Vietnam,[7] the initial Afghan strategy of the United States was to use a CIA developed plan to conduct irregular warfare in collusion with the Northern Alliance against the Taliban.[8] Similarly, a Joint, Interagency, Intergovernmental, Multinational (JIIM) perspective of the current tensions in sub-Saharan Africa, particularly the Central African Republic, South Sudan, and Mali compare to the Salvadoran Civil War, particularly the porous borders, human rights violations, transnational actors and influences, and the weakness and corruption of the mechanisms of governance. Open source documents from USAFRICOM describe the operational approach to the nation of Mali as containing elements of state

---

[7]Ronald Spector, *Advise and Support: The Early Years, 1941-1960* (Washington, DC: Center For Military History, 1983), 86-89.

[8]Steve Coll, *Ghost Wars: The Secret History of the CIA, Afghanistan and Bin Laden From the Soviet Invasion to September 10, 2001* (New York: Penguin, 2004), 15-16.

development and rule of law improvement as a higher priority than classic military-to-military development efforts, or foreign military sales (FMS) programs.[9]

Research Architecture

Explaining the differences between Vietnam and El Salvador as individual conflicts, and within the arc of the American war experience, would not be difficult. Describing the similarities, normalizing for variables, and synthesizing applicable lessons to take forward is both the challenge, and the purpose of this monograph. Section Two of this work describes the methodology of the study, and the literature applicable on the many facets of this study. This literature ranges from the historical works regarding both El Salvador and Vietnam conflicts, various theoretical and doctrinal works regarding irregular and counterinsurgent warfare, and the variety of theoretical models. Although the methodology ascribed to US Army Field Manual 3-24 *Counterinsurgency* (2006) nests well with the recently published ADRP 3.07 *Stability Operations* (2013), but a better comprehension of the pervasive nature of an insurgency is required.[10] FM 3-24 and ADRP 3.07 enable an operational planner to orchestrate tactical actions once an insurgency is in full bloom, but little in the way of doctrine exists to identify and treat the symptoms of an insurgency at its genesis.

Noted counterinsurgent theorists David Galula, Roger Trinquier, Mao Tse-tung, and Anthony Joes provide insight and perspective to this study. Consolidating input from these

---

[9]F. William Engdahl, "The War in Mali and AFRICOM's Agenda: Target China," *Global Research*, http://www.globalresearch.ca/the-war-in-mali-and-africoms-african-agenda-target-china/5322517 (accessed 15 February 2014).

[10]Department of the Army, Army Doctrine Publication (ADP) 3-07, *Stability* (Washington, DC: Government Printing Office, 15 February 2013), 3, 6-8. 13-14, http://armypubs.army.mil/doctrine/ DR_pubs/dr_a/pdf/adp3_07.pdf) (accessed 5 August 2013); Department of the Army, Field Manual (FM) 3-24, *Counterinsurgency* (Washington, DC: Government Printing Office, 15 December 2006), 3-31 – 3-33, https://armypubs.us.army.mil/ doctrine/ DR_pubs/dr_a/pdf/fm3_24.pdf) (accessed 8 August 2013).

notable theorists, this monograph will expand upon their principal theories in Section Two, with a review of contemporary U.S. Army and Joint Doctrine that is applicable in the study of counterinsurgency and stability operations. Section Three discusses Gordon McCormick's Diamond Model of insurgency. This is a highly effective tool to both frame the extent and growth of an insurgency in a particular operational area, and to devise an operational approach along JIIM lines of operation to identify, retard, and potentially defeat insurgent extent and growth patterns. McCormick's Model focuses on the mechanisms of state or counter-state (insurgent) social control and the sequencing of friendly tactical actions in an effort to gain a position of relative advantage. [11]

In Section Four, this study analyses the early stages of the Vietnam conflict using a case study methodology. Applicable to both Vietnam and El Salvador, the focal points of the analysis include: the history of conflict; the genesis of American involvement; the evolution of American involvement; the advised element, successes and failures; conflict denouement, and analysis relative to McCormick's Diamond Model. The discussion includes American influences in the early stages of the war, principally between the establishments of the Military Advisory Assistance Group (MAAG) in 1950, until its absorption into the Military Assistance Command-Vietnam (MAC-V) in 1963. [12] This case study focuses on the emphasis placed on military advisorship aimed at the Brigade, Division and Corps levels of the Army of South Vietnam

---

[11]Greg Wilson, "The Mystic Diamond: Applying the Diamond Model of Counterinsurgency in the Philippines," in *Gangs and Guerrillas: Ideas from Counterinsurgency and Counterterrorism*, ed. Michael Freeman and Hy Rothstein (Monterey: Naval Postgraduate School, 2011), 27-32, http://www.google.com/url?sa=t&rct=j&q=&esrc=s&source=web &cd=1&ved=0CCsQFjAA&url=http%3A%2F%2Fwww.nps.edu%2FAcademics%2FSchools%2 FGSOIS%2FDepartments%2FDA%2FDocuments%2FG%2520%26%2520G%25204_21_2011.p df&ei=Gd09U4OqBvfesASQ1IHgBQ&usg=AFQjCNF28kuIxYbqUede8t (accessed 5 January 2014).

[12]Graham Cosmas, *MACV: The Joint Command in the Years of Escalation 1962-1967* (Washington, DC: Government Printing Office, 2006), 42-43.

(ARVN), and the dearth of synchronized advisorship effort placed at the ministerial level of the South Vietnam government. This study also pays particular attention on the reciprocal approaches of targeting intermediaries of social control.

Section Five is devoted to the case study of the El Salvadoran Civil War, a multi-faceted conflict that persisted between 1979 and 1992. Unlike Vietnam, the United States focused less on directly influencing the tactical units in the field, and focused on a more balanced, JIIM approach, eventually working with the ministerial level of government to address the root causes of the insurgency. These efforts built toward a conflict resolution that, while resulting in a coalition government, provided for a level of prosperity and security for the preceding two decades. How the Government of El Salvador (GOES) was able to bolster its mechanisms of social control while targeting the FMLN intermediaries is key to this study.

Section Six analyses both conflicts, and proffers a conclusion to the contemporary operational planner. In reviewing the source data for both conflicts, the reader will quickly see patterns emerging within the operational approaches of the opposing forces. These patterns, when viewed through McCormick's Diamond Model, form a vision of insurgent forces as "forces in building". Both the El Salvador and Vietnam conflicts demonstrate these patterns, and demonstrate the strength of the McCormick Model. This study demonstrates a relationship between prioritizing operational effort to increase the effectiveness of state control mechanisms and the eventual success of a counterinsurgent conflict, at a lesser cost in American blood and treasure.

METHODOLOGY

An insurgency is a *protracted struggle* conducted methodologically, step by step, in order to attain specific intermediate objectives leading finally to the overthrow of the existing order. [13]

—David Galula, 1964

Roger Trinquier professed warnings of "Modern War" following his experiences in Indochina and Algeria. He defined it as conflict conducted not only among the populace as a passive audience, but conflict against politically empowered members of society who use elements of politics to wage indirect war against the state system.[14] A comparative case study model examining Vietnam and El Salvador adequately explores this topic, particularly the American advisory efforts undertaken in support of each respective state.[15] Using McCormick's Diamond Model to assess the relative operational approaches between the combatants, we can isolate the crucial variables of advisory effort between the two conflicts.

Vietnam escalated slowly into a conflict that eventually cost nearly 60,000 Americans their lives; El Salvador never attained a sustained American military presence that rarely exceeded 55 military personnel in the country.[16] When a long-term view of stability is applied,

---

[13]David Galula, *Counterinsurgency Warfare: Theory and Practice (Psi Classics of the Counterinsurgency Era)* (Westport: Praeger, 2006), 2-3.

[14]Roger Trinquier, *Modern Warfare: a French View of Counterinsurgency,* trans. from the French by Daniel Lee with an introduction by Bernard B. Fall, and foreword by Eliot A. Cohen (Westport, CT: Praeger, 2006), 7-8.

[15]Stephen Van Evera, *Guide to Methods for Students of Political Science* (Ithaca: Cornell University Press, 1997), 55-58.

[16]Kalev Sepp, "Best Practices in Counterinsurgency," *Military Review* (May-June 2005): 8-12, http://www.google.com/url?sa=t&rct=j&q=&esrc=s&source=web&cd= 1&ved= 0CCYQFjAA&url=http%3A%2F%2Fwww.au.af.mil%2Fau%2Fawc%2Fawcgate%2Fmilreview %2Fsepp.pdf&ei=H-09U6zcEcutsASZjYCYCg&usg= AFQjCNFjZWHBxdk Acti4gaRFphr4NkL6XQ&bvm=bv.64125504,d.cWc (accessed 29 December 2013), 10-11; Andrew Bacevich et al., *American Military Policy in Small Wars: The Case of El Salvador* (Washington, DC: Pergamon-Brassey's, 1988), 16-17.

both countries have normalized relations regionally, and are on a path to being productive members of the international community. Initial impressions indicate that the crucial variable may not be merely the amount of foreign effort applied to each conflict, but the precise targeting of advisor efforts at the national and subnational levels of governance as the key discriminator in the lack of escalation experienced in El Salvador.

While counterinsurgency literature has expanded exponentially since the end of World War II, this is not exclusively a study in counterinsurgency. This study does apply an aspect of the methodology used to define the scope of the military problem at the time when elements of American hard power were committed to the regions in conflict. Namely, what indicators of the breadth and depth of the insurgent threat were visible to regional planners, how did they formulate an operational approach for those initial phases of involvement, and how did they resource and prioritize the respective theaters of Vietnam and El Salvador? The academic and military reader gain greater insight into both this decision cycle, and the operational context wherein leaders made said decisions.

<u>Theory</u>

There exists an abundance of counterinsurgency warfare literature in today's academic environment. To analyze America's early involvement in Vietnam and El Salvador, contemporary and classic sources of information are required to place actions into context. David Galula in *Counter-insurgency Warfare* (1964) is the quintessential text from which the author will determine good and bad practices and traits exhibited by American, Vietnamese, and El Salvadoran COIN operators. Anthony Joes in *Resisting Rebellion* (2006) adds to the body of knowledge with his contemporary and historic case studies. Roger Trinquier and *Modern Warfare: a French View of Counterinsurgency* (1964) concludes these highlighted theorists, though this study includes the work of contemporary theorists and research institutions.

One salient point throughout the body of literature is that a successful counter-insurgent campaign requires a 'whole of government' approach. In analysis of Algeria and Vietnam, Roger Trinquier identifies the insurgents' approaches as similarly holistic, "…an interlocking system of actions—political, economic, psychological, military—that aims at the *overthrow of the established authority in a country and its replacement by another regime.*"[17] What is not clear in the example of an expeditionary counter-insurgent effort, such as NATO forces in Afghanistan from 2007-2014, is what agency from the American executive branch is responsible to synchronize and provide the non-military aspects of a COIN effort. Joint and Army doctrine attempts to bridge that gap.

Doctrine

The United States military's foundational doctrine is Joint Publication (JP) 3.0, *Joint Operations* (2011) and JP 5.0, *Joint Operation Planning* (2011). Key to understanding the current doctrinal sequencing of counterinsurgency operations lies in the joint phasing construct. A sequential progression through the six phases of the doctrinal Joint Operational Phasing Construct (Shape, Deter, Seize the Initiative, Dominate, Stabilize, Enable Civil Authority) may not be required if an insurgency is recognized and approached in the earlier Phase 0 and Phase 1. Phase 0 (Shape) of an operation is defined as: "Joint and multinational operations— inclusive of normal and routine military activities—and various interagency activities are performed to dissuade or deter potential adversaries and to assure or solidify relationships with friends and allies." JP 5.0 identifies Phase 1 of an operation as Deter: "The intent of this phase is to deter undesirable adversary action by demonstrating the capabilities and resolve of the joint force. It includes activities to prepare forces and set conditions for deployment and employment of forces in the

---

[17]Trinquier, *Modern Warfare*, 6 (emphasis in original).

event that deterrence is not successful."[18] A risk exists of misapplication of combat power in the Seize the Initiative (Phase 2) and Dominate (Phase 3) operations. A heavy-handed approach can create distance between the populace and the state, and add to the grievances that fostered the insurgencies initial inception and growth.[19]

The contemporary Army Capstone Doctrine exists in ADP 3.0, *Unified Land Operations* (2011), while the current counterinsurgent doctrine resides in FM 3-24, *Counterinsurgency*. Placing both the Salvadoran Civil War and Vietnam conflict into a contemporary paradigm, this monograph will also refer to ADP 3-07 *Stability* as nested doctrine within the Wide Area Security (WAS) mission set described in *Unified Land Operations* (ULO).[20]

History-Doctrine-Theory Synthesis

Anthony Joes describes the catalysts and complexity of a third-world wide area security (WAS) environment, and mirrors both the doctrinaires and other theorists in attempting to operationalize Stability Operations (STABOPS) and counterinsurgent theories. Joes spends considerable effort describing the historic usage of host-nation security forces, and emphasizes the United States successes and failures with regard to the early development of the Army of

---

[18]Chairman, Joint Chiefs of Staff, Joint Publication (JP) 5-0, *Joint Operations Planning* (Washington, DC: Government Printing Office, 2011), xxiii-xxiv. A friction that a combatant commander may struggle with is that by the time, a COIN struggle has reached a threshold of committing American or allied forces, a host nation governance may be at the point of collapsing from the insurgents' efforts. Shaping and Deterrence efforts, oriented toward monolithic resistance movements or conventional adversaries, may have failed, and the command must immediately move into Phase IV, Stabilize. "The stabilize phase is required when there is no fully functional, legitimate civil governing authority present. The joint force may be required to perform limited local governance, integrating the efforts of other supporting/ contributing multinational, IGO, NGO, or USG agency participants until legitimate local entities are functioning," xxiv.

[19]David Kilcullen, *Counterinsurgency* (New York: Oxford University Press, 2010), 3.

[20]Department of the Army, ADP 3-07, *Stability*, 8-9.

South Vietnam (ARVN).[21] He also discusses successful strategies of finding peaceable paths to social change, and notes how open elections in Malaya and during the Philippine Hukbalahap rebellion were the *coup de grace* in successful COIN campaigns, as they were in El Salvador. Similar to Galula[22] and Sun Tzu,[23] Joes' comments on the positive effects of reconciliation and repatriation with a number of examples, most notably Abraham Lincoln offering full amnesty to the Southern states and curtailing a likely guerrilla conflict, there is only one small reference to the topic of reconciliation in the reviewed ULO doctrine.[24] Capturing many of the same lessons learned from the preceding centuries of low-intensity conflict, Anthony Joes' theories significantly impact the ULO doctrine, and play a key part in the analysis of the Salvadoran Civil War, and the Vietnam conflict.

The works of David Galula and Roger Trinquier play heavily into the doctrinal aspects of STABOPS and WAS. Most noticeable are their theories of the long-term and methodical manner of insurgent growth, the primacy of the military over the political aspects of a campaign, the criticality of maintaining the initiative, and the mechanisms on both sides (state and anti-state) that foster the growth or destruction of insurgent forces and ideations. Galula remarks on the protracted nature of an insurgency, and the methodological execution of it by the leadership of the insurgency. Mao Tse-tung remarked upon the protracted nature of an insurgency,[25] as did Greg

---

[21]Anthony James Joes, *Resisting Rebellion: The History of Politics and Counterinsurgency* (Lexington, KY: University of Kentucky Press, 2006), 135-36; Department of the Army, FM 3-24, *Counterinsurgency,* 8-9—8-11.

[22]Galula, *Counterinsurgency Warfare: Theory and Practice*, 52-53.

[23]Sun Tzu, *The Art of War,* trans. Samuel B. Griffith (New York: Oxford University Press, 1963), 76.

[24]Joes, *Resisting Rebellion: The History of Politics and Counterinsurgency*, 233-24, 237-38; Department of the Army, FM 3-24, *Counterinsurgency,* 5-12—5-13.

[25]Mao Tse-Tung, *Mao Tse-Tung On the Protracted War* (Beijing: Foreign Languages Press, 1960), 26.

Wilson in his observations of the early American campaign in the Philippines as a part of Operation Enduring Freedom.[26] The heavy emphasis in ADP 3-07 on the civil aspects of stability operations is mirrored by Galula's emphasis on the end goal of a STABOPS campaign, namely that, "What is at stake is the country's political regime, and to defend it is a political affair. Even if this requires military action, the action is consistently directed toward a political goal…the military action is secondary to the political one."[27]

The tasks attributed to WAS by ADP 3.0, and the primary Army stability tasks listed in ADP 3-07 are nearly identical, and describe a population-centric aspect of framing a JIIM response to a crisis. ADP 3-07 describes the Army stability tasks as: establish civil security; establish civil control; restore essential services; support to governance, and; support to economic and infrastructure development.[28] ADRP 3.0 discusses wide area security and initiative, guiding commanders and staffs to: improve civil conditions; identify and pursue nonmilitary objectives, such as effective governance, reconstruction, and public safety, and; work with civil partners to remedy conditions affecting property and domestic order. The emphasized tasks in WAS and STABOPS draw heavily from historic and contemporary writings on population security and control as a necessary factor to success in a counterinsurgent operation or campaign, and this begins with the earliest mechanisms of state formation.[29]

---

[26]Gregory Wilson, "Anatomy of a Successful COIN Operation: OEF-Philippines and the Indirect Approach," *Military Review* 86, no. 6 (November-December 2006): 2.

[27]Galula, *Counterinsurgency Warfare: Theory and Practice,* 89; Department of the Army, ADP 3-07, *Stability*, 11-12.

[28]Department of the Army, ADP 3-07, *Stability*, 11.

[29]Department of the Army, Army Doctrine Publication (ADP) 3-0, *Unified Land Operations* (Washington, DC: Government Printing Office, 2011), http://armypubs.army.mil/doctrine/DR_pubs/dr_a/pdf/adp3_0.pdf (accessed 5 August 2013), 2.2.

While not solely an American construct, the military as subordinate to their civil leadership also supports this principle, especially if a component of WAS or STABOPS involves conducting Foreign Internal Defense (FID), either with conventional or special forces.[30] Mentorship by example is a powerful tool to use when conducting partnered operations; it can apply to weapons discipline, vehicular maintenance, and espousing ideals of the Western construct of civil-military relationships. Analysis of mentorship efforts in both Vietnam and El Salvador is a key component to this monograph. Adopting a professional, well-resourced approach to advisement has a value in STABOPS, and when using advisors to bolster a nascent counterinsurgent campaign can mean victory or defeat.[31]

CONTROL, COUNTERINSURGENCY AND MCCORMICK'S DIAMOND MODEL

> The communists had killed about 10,000 village chiefs in a country that has 16,000 villages. This…is "control"—not the military illusion of it.[32]
>
> —Bernard Fall, 1960

The strength of an insurgency is maintaining its cloak of invisibility to the agents of the state (the counterinsurgent force). An operational planner that understands the mechanisms of power of a state will soon be able to frame an environment, and an operational approach, that identifies the vacuum of state control in order to penetrate an insurgency's invisibility.[33] In

---

[30]Chairman, Joint Chiefs of Staff, Joint Publication (JP) 3-22, *Foreign Internal Defense 12 July 2010* (Washington, DC: Government Printing Office, 2012), x-xi.

[31]Lujan, *Light Footprints*, 30, 35.

[32]Bernard Fall, *The Two Viet-Nams: A Political and Military Analysis* (New York: Praeger, 1967), 52.

[33]Brian Greenshields, "Population Control," in *Gangs and Guerrillas: Ideas from Counterinsurgency and Counterterrorism*, ed. Michael Freeman and Hy Rothstein (Monterey: Naval Postgraduate School, 2011), 77-81, http://www.google.com/url?sa=t&rct=j&q=&esrc= s&source=web&cd=1&ved=0CCsQFjAA&url =http%3A%2F%2Fwww.nps.edu%2FAcademics %2FSchools%2FGSOIS%2FDepartments%2FDA%2FDocuments%2FG%2520%26%2520G%2 5204_21_2011.pdf&ei=Gd09U4OqBvfesASQ1IHgBQ&usg=AFQjCNF28kuIxYbqUede8t (accessed 5 January 2014).

discussing the latter days of the French Indochina War and the efforts of the Vietminh, Bernard Fall described this vacuum of state control as a *de facto* signpost pointing to insurgent zones of geographic occupation.[34]

Wilson discussed the methodological aspects of insurgent growth patterns, and the mechanisms of the state that are targeted or co-opted by the insurgent to extend control over the populace, a topic that both Galula and Fall reference with regard to the Indochina War of 1946-1954. [35] Particular examples used were that of the assassinations or disappearances of Saigon-appointed village chieftains and schoolteachers, and the presence or absence of tax income as an indicator of Vietminh influence.[36] Charles Tilly discusses the ties between the mechanisms of the state that emerge as a result of the state participating in conflict, namely those extractive mechanisms to provide monies for conflict, and those controlling functions that coerce a population to provide representatives for conscripted service.[37] The insurgent has extractive desires upon the populace as well, because his growth mechanism secures more guns, money, and bodies for the insurgent effort. Wilson's article, and McCormick's course at the Naval Postgraduate School, "Seminar in Guerrilla Warfare," place particular emphasis on the sub-national mechanisms of social control and extraction as the true battlefield in a counterinsurgent campaign, and require further exposition.[38]

---

[34]Fall, *The Two Viet-Nams*, 50-53.

[35]Wilson, "Anatomy of a Successful COIN Operation," 3.

[36]Galula, *Counterinsurgency Warfare*, 18-20, 52; Joes, *Resisting Rebellion*, 37-39.

[37]Charles Tilly, *Coercion, Capital and European States: AD 990-1992* (Cambridge: Blackwell, 1990), 122-126.

[38]Wilson, "The Mystic Diamond: Applying the Diamond Model of Counterinsurgency in the Philippines," 17; Gordon McCormick, "Seminar in Guerrilla Warfare," lecture series (Monterey, CA: Naval Postgraduate School, July-September, 2009).

American Doctrine and Control

The Diamond Model draws heavily from McCormick's research into guerrilla and insurgent warfare, both Marxist and Maoist in origin, and draws heavily from Galula, Trinquier, and Mao Tse-tung. McCormick based the model largely on his personal research into the Peruvian Shining Path insurgency in the 1980s and 1990s. He begins with the hypothesis that insurgencies do not happen randomly, winning or losing a counterinsurgent fight is not a function of randomness, and there exists a predictable and analytical nature to an insurgency.[39] This predictability affects both the insurgent, and "the state" (the term refers to both the mechanisms of the affected nation-state, and the counter-insurgent force), and rests upon the zero-sum game aspect of control. The theories espoused by both Galula and Trinquier echo this methodological manner of growth. JP 5-0 defines "control" as both a verb and a noun:

> Control. To establish public order and safety, securing borders, routes, sensitive sites, population centers, and individuals and physically occupying key terrain and facilities. As a stability mechanism, control closely relates to the primary stability task, establish civil control. However, control is also fundamental to effective, enduring security. When combined with the stability mechanism compel, it is inherent to the activities that comprise disarmament, demobilization, and reintegration, as well as broader security sector reform programs. Without effective control, efforts to establish civil order—including efforts to establish both civil security and control over an area and its population—will not succeed. Establishing control requires time, patience, and coordinated, cooperative efforts across the OA [Operational Area].[40]

Theory and Control

Tilly defines a nation-state as "coercion-wielding organizations that ... exercise clear priority in some respects over all other organizations within substantial territories."[41] He also holds that war created the state system of internal bureaucratic processes, extractive taxation

---

[39]McCormick, "Seminar in Guerrilla Warfare"; Trinquier, *Modern Warfare*, 8-9.

[40]Chairman, Joint Chiefs of Staff, Joint Publication (JP) 5.0, *Operations Planning*, III-30 (Washington, DC: Government Printing Office). Parenthetical added by author for clarity.

[41]Tilly, *Coercion, Capital, and European States, AD 990-1992*, 1.

mechanisms, and the gradual codification and legitimacy of the coercive use of force to maintain the authority of the state.[42] The operational level planner involved in WAS or STABOPS must place the essential functions of the host nation governance into this coercive mechanism context. While Tilly's historical base was the evolution of the European models of state evolution, his theory is still viable when held against other regional states of interest. Though a single layer of analysis may produce a binomial answer ("Is it European, or not?"), a deeper analysis that accounts for colonial history, tribal or ethnic social evolution, or historic regional conflicts (and their subsequent effects on the host nation infrastructure) may add to the planner's understanding of one aspect of the situation. With retrospective view, both the Vietnam and El Salvador conflicts have, at their base, deep ties to frictions created by overlaying colonial efforts on top of existing ethnic tensions. With knowledge of the genesis of the foreign bureaucratic morass that an operational planner has found, the planner can now begin to frame a solution to reestablishing a semblance of social control. McCormick's Model begins to form as elements of Approach 2 begin to coalesce conceptually against an operational environment.[43]

Intermediaries in the McCormick equation—tax collectors, schoolteachers, clergy, municipal governance, judges, and the *petit* bureaucracy, exercise state control. State control applies to terrain, installations, institutions, key individuals, media, and populace.[44] Retaining control of its sovereign territory and populace is one of the prerequisites of successful statehood, and requires investment of time, money, and professionalization efforts. The coercive power of the state initially forces endogenous control on its members. As time progresses and the state

---

[42]Ibid., 187.

[43]Brian Taylor and Roxana Botea, "Tilly Tally: War-Making and State-Making in the Contemporary Third World," *International Studies Review* 10, no. 1 (2008): 27-56, 28-29; Galula, *Counterinsurgency Warfare,* 25-26.

[44]Greg Wilson, "The Mystic Diamond: Applying the Diamond Model of Counterinsurgency in the Philippines," 28-29; McCormick, "Seminar in Guerrilla Warfare."

increasingly meets the needs of the populace, the constituency internalizes the original outcomes of the coercive power of the state as the mores, folkways, and rules of a society.[45]

Charles Tilly may not have the perfect model solution for state control in the Third World for the WAS planner to use, but his emphasis on the temporal aspects of state control are critical. Brian Taylor and Roxana Botea comment upon Tillyan theory in regards to their case studies of Afghanistan and Vietnam, two non-European countries with decade's long conflicts against endogenous and exogenous threats. FM 3-24, *Counterinsurgency*, a companion manual to Unified Land Operations, advocates such deeper environmental analysis coupled with a long-term temporal assessment.[46] A rapid reading of a mission analysis slide may pass by the salient points of Taylor and Botea's argument, namely the time-indexed ethnographic aspects of a crisis area.

European states eventually coalesced around common languages and ethnicities, and formed as functions of raising monies, building armies, and making states through war. Taylor and Botea identify two catalysts that lead to nation building in the third world. The first is the strong ethnocentric core that was the traditional leader in the past, and the second is a civil or regional war that forced the leadership to create and use a strong national ideology.[47] In this example, the externally created nation of North Vietnam, though communist at its base, flourished as a state following the decades of war from 1946 to 1975 due to its monolithic ethnology, and the blending of communist ideology with fervent nationalism.[48] Afghanistan, despite a similar period of war, has not thrived despite the state of continual war from 1978 to 2013, largely due to the exact inverse of the Vietnamese condition. El Salvador has reached a

_____

[45]McCormick, "Seminar in Guerrilla Warfare."

[46]FM 3-24, *Counterinsurgency,* 1-22–1-25.

[47]Taylor and Botea, "Tilly Tally," 29-30.

[48]Harry Summers, *On Strategy: A Critical Analysis of the Vietnam War* (New York: Presidio Press, 1995), 17-18.

tenuous peace only through power and wealth sharing initiatives, near-homogeneous

ethnography, and a noteworthy post-conflict reconciliation program among the combatants that

has actually strengthened state institutions of social control.[49]

McCormick's Diamond

McCormick's Diamond Model begins with three axioms. If a planner holds these as

truths, the remainder of the model logically follows:

1. The state is a force in being, and that the insurgency is a force in development.
2. Each side has an opening advantage—the state has the advantage of force, and the insurgency has the advantage of information.
3. The first side in a counterinsurgency fight to overcome their initial disadvantage wins the conflict.[50]

For either of the contending sides, the Clausewitzian center of gravity is control of the

population.[51] This is decisive for the insurgent, because control of the population bequeaths

further people (recruits), guns and money for the insurgent element. An insurgency must increase

in size and territory to gain success. Conversely, the decisive point for the state is also the control

of the population. Control of the population produces both information about the insurgent force,

and support for the state's continuing existence and legitimacy.[52]

Within McCormick's Model, there are only three operational approaches that are

available to each side of the insurgency fight. The graphic below depicts the approaches relative

to the center of gravity, and the other actors. These approaches indicate the possible nature of a

counterinsurgent campaign. The simplest form of McCormick's Model is a triangle, obviating the

---

[49]Taylor and Botea, "Tilly Tally," 56.

[50]Wilson, "The Mystic Diamond: Applying the Diamond Model of Counterinsurgency in the Philippines," 15; McCormick, "Seminar in Guerrilla Warfare."

[51]Clausewitz, *On War*, 596-97; FM 3-24, *Counterinsurgency*, 3-14; Harry Summers, *On Strategy*, 128-29.

[52]Tilly, *Coercion, Capital, and European States*, 16-17, 26.

"international actors" from the diamond, rolling expeditionary counterinsurgent elements under the rubric of "the state." For the early stages of Vietnam, and the El Salvador Civil War, this simplification is effective in discerning validity of the base hypothesis.[53]

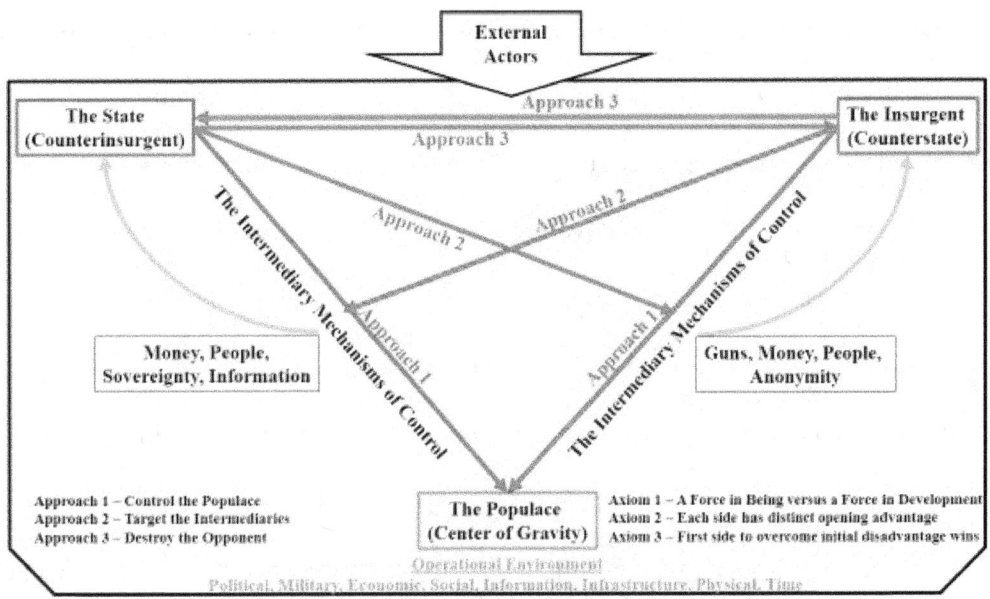

Figure 1: McCormick's (modified) Diamond Model[54]

Source: McCormick, "Seminar in Guerrilla War," Naval Postgraduate School, August 2009.

---

[53]McCormick, "Seminar in Guerrilla Warfare"; Coll, *Ghost Wars*, 85-88, 93-97. Complex environments, such as the interplay of the competing approaches between the Mujahedeen, the Democratic Republic of Afghanistan (DRA), the USSR, the USA, Pakistan, the Inter-services Intelligence Agency of Pakistan (ISI), Saudi Arabia, and China during the Soviet-Afghanistan War of 1979-1988 rapidly creates a geometric pattern of approaches requiring analysis that would supersede the mandate of this monograph.

[54]Wilson represents this graphically in his two articles, and is recreated here from the author's notes from "Seminar in Guerrilla War" in the Naval Postgraduate School, August 2009. The author has taken the liberty to modify the basic architecture, removing the "international actors" and their relative operational approaches, for clarity's sake, while also placing the populace in a symbolic tipping point locale within the model.

Within the simplified triangle model, the state and the insurgents stand alone, with the population spread before them. For simplicity's sake, "the state" is the core element of a Westphalian nation state's ruling body, and the regime that it surrounds itself with which to promulgate and retain its power.[55] "The insurgent" contains the ideological core of the element, and the apex leadership and administrative elements that have established themselves as a counter-state. For this model, expeditionary stabilizing forces from third countries (e.g., British Commonwealth forces in the Malay Peninsula in 1955), or third nation reinforcing efforts (e.g., American Office of Strategic Services (OSS) elements in Vichy France in 1943) are grouped with "the state" and "the insurgent," respectively. The insurgent has its mechanisms to control the population (enforcement agents, tax collectors, military recruiters, political and educational cadres, judges, logistical acquisition and distribution, etc.), and the state has similar agents that operate between it and the people (police, district/provincial governance, ministers, civil servants, schoolteachers, jurisprudence systems, etc.).[56] The operational approaches logically are:

1. Control the population. For the insurgent, this gains more people, guns and money, so they grow bigger, which lets them move geographically to new villages, generating more people, guns and money. Incrementally, this enables the insurgent eventually to overcome their initial disadvantage, Axiom 2. For the state, controlling the population offsets the informational advantage that the insurgent has at the opening of the conflict, and refers to the zero sum game of population control.

2. Target the intermediate agents. The insurgent, as he consolidates power in one area, will mass his efforts, use his informational superiority, and attack the representatives of the state in that area. Conversely, as the state consolidates power in an area, the population feels less under the control of the insurgent, and is more willing to provide information about the insurgent, allowing the state to target the insurgent's mechanisms of social control.

3. Target directly the strategic apex. Push either the insurgent or the state past a breaking point. The state reaches its breaking point when the insurgency has grown

---

[55]Colin Gray, *Another Bloody Century: Future Warfare* (London: Phoenix, 2005), 66.

[56]Wilson, "The Mystic Diamond: Applying the Diamond Model of Counterinsurgency in the Philippines," 16; McCormick, "Seminar in Guerrilla Warfare".

so large that it controls nearly everything in the country, save for the capital. The insurgency reaches its breaking point when the state controls so much of the country that the insurgent has lost the informational advantage.[57]

Sequencing and synchronicity of the operational approaches in McCormick's Model are key. At the onset, the state, though blind to the insurgent's efforts, has a force advantage and is a force in existence, whereas the insurgent has an information advantage, and is weak, a force in development (Axiom 1). The first side to overcome the opening disadvantage wins (Axiom 3). Logically, the operational approach would follow a sequence of Approach 1, Approach 2, then Approach 3, with a reasonable level of simultaneity as the operational environment evolves proportional to the energy injected into the system of the insurgency. The threat to the state is the political or egoistical urge to fix the problem now and pursue Approach 3 at the onset of a conflict, which potentially leads to operational overreach, or human rights violations, such as the Salvadoran massacre of a civilian population at El Mozote in December 1981.[58] Similarly, when the insurgent seeks to target the apex of the state before attaining the quasi-conventional mass required, such as in the Tet Offensive of 1968, the superior force of the state sees and neutralizes the fighting elements of the insurgency.[59]

The Vietnam and El Salvador case studies will follow similar patterns to describe the relative strengths and weaknesses of the echelon of respective mentorship focus. The genesis of the American involvement will follow a brief history of the conflict. In each case, an evolution of American involvement is notable in the literature, and shapes the argument of both appropriate echeloning of advisorship, and effectiveness of the advised elements relative to McCormick's

---

[57]Wilson, "The Mystic Diamond: Applying the Diamond Model of Counterinsurgency in the Philippines," 16-17; McCormick, "Seminar in Guerrilla Warfare".

[58]Mark Danner, *Massacre at El Mozote, A Parable of the Cold War* (New York: Vintage, 1994), 67-77; Trinquier, *Modern Warfare*, 56-60.

[59]Philip Davidson, *Vietnam at War: The History 1946-1975* (New York: Oxford University Press, 1991), 499-503; Andrew Krepinevich, *The Army and Vietnam*, 238-9.

Diamond Model. The author will dedicate effort to describing the various advised elements

within each foreign military, and the appropriate successes and failures that ultimately led to a

denouement of each conflict.

VIETNAM CASE STUDY

> The Armed Forces of the Soviet Union structured, equipped and trained their
> forces for nuclear and high-intensity war on the great northern European plain and the
> plains of northern China. However, their political leadership thrust them into the middle
> of the Afghanistan civil war to reconstitute and support a nominally Marxist-Leninist
> government. The terrain, the climate and the enemy were entirely different from what
> they had prepared for. In this locale, their equipment functioned less than optimally, their
> force structure was clearly inappropriate and their tactics were obviously wrong. [60]
> —Les Grau, 1998

The conflict in French Indochina did not begin for America in June 1966 with the

infusion of 44 American combat battalions to the country of South Vietnam.[61] By this stage in the

game, American advisors and support troops had been assisting the fledgling democracy, and

their former French masters, since 1944. Following the French defeat at Dien Bien Phu on 7 May

1954, and the subsequent division of the area into communist North Vietnam, and democratic

South Vietnam, America assumed the exclusive mantel of armament and advisorship

responsibility for the south.[62] What followed was a combined Department of State and

Department of Defense effort to both increase the size of and to modernize the military, while

simultaneously manipulating the governance in Saigon to increase pro-Western leanings. The

---

[60]Lester Grau, *The Bear Went Over the Mountain: Soviet Combat Tactics in Afghanistan* (Portland: Frank Cass Publishers, 1998), xvii.

[61]Krepinevich, *The Army and Vietnam,* 3; John A. Nagl and Peter J. Schoomaker, *Learning to Eat Soup with a Knife: Counterinsurgency Lessons from Malaya and Vietnam* (Chicago: The University of Chicago Press, 2005), 150-151. President Johnson decided, based on emerging requirements and GEN Westmoreland (Commander, MAC-V) to commit 44 battalions of combat power (Army and U.S. Marine Corps) to South Vietnam in July of 1965. By June 1966, all battalions were present in South Vietnam and had completed Reception, Staging, Onward Movement and Integration (RSOI).

[62]Lind, *Vietnam: The Necessary War,* 9-11.

purpose, presumably, was to prevent the Korea-like large-scale war, which was on the horizon, from happening and the resultant collapse of Indochina into the global Communism sphere of influence.

The advisor effort failed primarily because of a lack of unity of effort, a lack of a clear operational approach, and a dogmatic vision of war that remained firmly gazing into both the rearview mirror at the Korean conflict, and at the American Army's structure, culture and doctrinal way of fighting.[63] It also failed because of a lack of sustained advisorship effort at the Ministry of Defense echelons, and Prime Minister Diem's fixation on consolidating and protecting his personal power following the French departure. Developing an American-style armed force without investing in counter-corruption and good governance efforts created an RVN military entity that focused on maintaining the regime in Saigon while furthering the political and personal ambitions of commanders.[64] This led to a failure of the counterinsurgent effort in the rural areas, and allowed the resurgent Vietminh, now labeled Vietcong, to secure money, guns, and manpower from the populace.[65] A focused advisorship effort of both civil and military actors at the national and subnational levels, coupled with a deeper analysis of the mechanics of an insurgency, could have prevented the massive escalation in the mid-1960s. Relative to McCormick's Model, the ARVN and the Saigon governance focused too heavily on pursuing Approach 2 (Target the Intermediate Agents) and Approach 3 (Target the Strategic Apex) with its heavy-handed techniques, while ignoring Approach 3 (Control the Population), an oversight that allowed the Vietcong insurgency to seize the neglected political and physical terrain, and blossom in size beyond control.

---

[63] Joes, *Resisting Rebellion*, 183-184.

[64] Sheehan, *A Bright Shining Lie*, 324-325.

[65] Sheehan, *A Bright Shining Lie*, 172-174; Joes, *Resisting Rebellion*, 38-39.

History of Conflict

The Indochina Peninsula was a region of conflict going back through recorded history, though the Japanese occupation during World War II gave rise to the bifurcated nature of the state of Vietnam, and the communist-backed Vietminh movement. France began its colonial operations of Vietnam in the 1850s, proceeding from Cambodia and southern Vietnam to the northern tier provinces and the Red River Valley in the 1880s. Pre-Pearl Harbor Japanese expansion through the Pacific, and metropolitan France's defeat at the hands of Germany in May 1940 led to an increased Japanese influence in the heavily populated eastern and southeastern areas of the Indochina Peninsula, namely Hue, Saigon and Haiphong.[66] As the United States entered the war and formed an alliance with Generalissimo Chiang Kai-shek of China, Allied strategic leaders viewed the Indochina Peninsula as key to the war effort, particularly as a line of communication to provide logistic support to China. The war progressed, and resistance movements against both the residual Vichy French colonial leadership and the encroaching Imperial Japanese forces rose, eventually giving rise to a nationalist leader named Ho Chi Minh, and the Vietminh insurgent group.[67]

Genesis of American Involvement

Following the liberation of metropolitan France in August of 1944, both French factions in Indochina, the Gaullists and the Vichy, could operate together with the American Office of Strategic Services (OSS) Detachment 202 in Southern China to resist Japanese pressure through the nascent resistance organizations.[68] The Japanese coup of March 1945 against the remaining

---

[66]Spector, *Advice and Assist*, 27.

[67]Fall, *The Two Viet-Nams*, 40-42.

[68]Spector, *Advice and Assist*, 29, 39.

French influence gave greater political space for the both breeds of nationalists, the anti-French, and the anti-Japanese, to align their efforts and grow in size and strength through both American and British efforts.[69]

As the world emerged from World War II, American strategic leaders identified a clear polarity of the post-war political milieu—the Communist influence was spreading, and the Western liberal democracies were on the defensive. Predating the pivotal National Security Council (NSC) Memorandum 68 by scant months, NSC 64 defined the Indochina Peninsula as key to the entirety of Southeast Asia, and gave first voice to the "Domino Theory" of the spread of communism through Asia and the Pacific.[70] NSC 68, approved by President Truman on 30 September 1950, identified the containment of Communism as an American strategic interest, and effectively enabled the Department of Defense to resource a large standing military outside of an open declaration of war with an opposing nation-state.[71] The American military response to this was slow at first, providing logistical support to the French as they sought to regain control of their former colonial state, while simultaneously attempting not to endorse the French colonial system.[72] To this end, the United States established the Military Assistance Advisory Group (MAAG) in September 1950, with BG Francis Bunk as its first commander.[73] This initial effort, managed through the American consulate in Saigon, also only supported the French forces, as opposed to developing a uniformed military service to represent the Emperor Bao Dai-led Vietnam. In 1950, the Vietnamese National Army consisted of only 16,000 Soldiers, largely led

---

[69]Spector, *Advice and Assist*, 30; Davidson, *Vietnam at War*, 25-27.

[70]Spector, *Advice and Assist*, 107.

[71]Walter McDougal, *Promised Land, Crusader State: The American Encounter with the World Since 1776* (Boston: Mariner Books, 1997), 165-66.

[72]Spector, *Advice and Assist*, 102.

[73]Spector, *Advice and Assist*, 111-115; Davidson, *Vietnam at War*, 292-93.

by French Army officers, and organized as a constabulary force. There were no higher-level staffs or headquarters.[74] Following the French defeat at Dien Bien Phu in 1954, participants in the Geneva peace accords nominally divided the country of Vietnam at the 17th Parallel into a communist, secular North, and a dynastic, Catholic South.[75] The French withdrew from Hanoi on 9 October 1954, and the Vietminh filled the vacuum left by their withdrawal.[76]

Each political side of Vietnam withdrew to their side of the Demilitarized Zone (DMZ) and began consolidating power. For the communist North, this involved conducting land reforms in a Maoist fashion, building the bureaucracy of an authoritarian state, and heavy industrialization and modernization efforts. Ho Chi Minh undertook these efforts, and included a rearmament campaign in collusion with Communist powerhouses China and the USSR.[77] The North did not lose sight of their conviction of one country of Vietnam, ruled by the Vietnamese. While the educated Catholic northerners fled to South Vietnam, hidden within these droves were former anti-French Vietminh, operatives, who if the supposed national elections went awry (or were cancelled, which was the future reality), would enable a long peoples' war in Maoist fashion.[78] In the summer of 1954, Prime Minister Ngo dinh Diem, following his appointment by Emperor Bao Dai, led the South Vietnam central government. Diem, born in 1901, was raised in the imperial courts of the traditional capital of Hue, and was of the privileged Mandarin class. He was also a staunch anti-Communist and semi-devout Roman Catholic, and had fought a series of suppressive

---

[74]Spector, *Advice and Assist*, 131.

[75]Ibid., 219.

[76]Davidson, *Vietnam at War*, 283.

[77]Ibid., 284-289.

[78]Neil Sheehan, *A Bright Shining Lie: John Paul Vann and America in Vietnam* (New York: Random House, 1988), 136-138, 185-186; Joes, *Resisting Rebellion*, 134-136; Krepinevich, *The Army and Vietnam*, 18-20.

fights against other political parties, securing his leadership of the dominant Can Lao Party.[79] Through a series of central governmental power exchanges, and intensive centralization of power emanating from the Catholic-dominated Saigon oligarchy, the predominately Buddhist population was increasingly disenfranchised from participating in governance.[80] The resultant unrest created a political vacuum across a vast area of rural southern Vietnam, and allowed the Vietcong to move freely about the physical and sub-national political space, acquiring guns, money, and members, and growing larger and more competent.[81]

Evolution of American Involvement

The military of South Vietnam was in a sad state of repair following the French Indochina War, and attempting to rebuild it in the image of the American Army without addressing larger civil-military issues was a recipe for failure. The genesis point of the Army of South Vietnam was the indigenous forces mounted by the French Colonial forces in response to Communist overtures following World War II. At the inception of the American advisory effort, the ARVN displayed a marked lack of professionalization, drawing its officers from the Catholic minority of the oligarchic political machine in the South.[82] Similar to El Salvador, there was a marginal non-commissioned officer cadre as a military backbone.[83]

---

[79]Edward G. Lansdale, *In the Midst of Wars: An American's Mission to Southeast Asia* (Fordham: Fordham University Press, 1991), 154-56; Spector, *Advice and Assist*, 346.

[80]Joes, *Resisting Rebellion*, 36-38; Lansdale, *In the Midst of Wars*, 152-153; Sheehan, *A Bright Shining Lie*, 334-335.

[81]Sheehan, *A Bright Shining Lie*, 100-101; Davidson, *Vietnam at War*, 289-91.

[82]Sheehan, *A Bright Shining Lie*, 141.

[83]Spector, *Advice and Assist*, 285-86.

The Advised Element

The period between the birth of South Vietnam in 1954 and the denouement of the American advisory effort of the ARVN forces in December 1963 was a time of remarkable growth of the ARVN. The progenitor of the ARVN, the Vietnamese National Army (VNA) grew from the earlier French-led formations, the *battalions Vietnamiens* (BVNS). In July of 1954, the Vietnamese National Army consisted of "82 BVN battalions, 81 light infantry battalions, five airborne battalions, six imperial guard battalions and nine artillery battalions, for a total of 167,700 regulars."[84] While Krepinevich notes the lack of midgrade leadership and helicopters as being key deficiencies, Galula would comment that the building blocks for a successful counterinsurgent force were present: "...infantry, and more infantry, highly mobile and lightly armed..."[85] The ratio of maneuver forces (infantry battalions) to artillery battalions supports Galula's postulate, and eliminates the ease with which counterinsurgents can choose to send a bullet, rather than a man.[86] Paramilitary forces also sustained a dearth of motivation, personnel strength, and equipment; the Self Defense Corps (SDC) and the Civil Guard (CG), being the closest to the populace, often in and around the Strategic Hamlets, were also among the most corrupt forces, exploiting the populace, and supporting the Vietcong. They did this directly, often with logistics or information, and indirectly, driving the population to the Vietcong through the corruptness of the paramilitary forces. By 1960, CG and SDC units were in such a state of disarray the MAAG, with ARVN leadership, often sent ARVN units to assist. Since this distracted the training and development programs for the ARVN, the Americans either provided trainers for the regional training centers, or contracted the service. From 1954-63, there were no

---

[84]Krepinevich, *The Army and Vietnam*, 21-22.

[85]Galula, *Counterinsurgency Warfare*, 65.

[86]Department of the Army, FM 3-24, *Counterinsurgency*, 7-7.

American advisors assigned specifically to mentor SDC or CG elements.[87] In the meantime, the National Liberation Front (NLF) of the Vietcong activated in South Vietnam, and continued generating guns, money and recruits among the rural areas while slaughtering the SDC and CG.[88]

The Force Development

American forces did experience a level of success with advising their ARVN counterparts, though these were limited to developing the institutions that built the force, as opposed to developing a force that was trained, capable and led to success in counterinsurgent operations. For security purposes, and due to the proximity of the highest population areas, the MAAG, working with the RVN defense establishment, placed the initial entry training depots in places such as Quang Trung and Nha Trang. As the advising mission progressed from 1955 into early 1960, the non-commissioned officers (NCO) schooling and the officer professional schooling establishments also contributed to the encirclement of Saigon.[89] Increased American money brought increases to small unit capabilities; radios, armored personnel carriers (APCs), helicopters, and artillery. By 1960, the MAAG created seven divisions of ARVN, and sought a corps-level exercise to validate the ARVN ability to defeat an armored thrust from North Vietnam.[90]

Joint Combined Arms Maneuver

Elements of the 7th ARVN Division conducted a complex air assault attack to destroy elements of the Vietcong 504th Main Force Battalion on 20-21 July 1962. The operation, while

---

[87]Krepinevich, *The Army in Vietnam*, 24-25; Spector, *Advice and Assist*, 363.

[88]Krepinevich, *The Army in Vietnam*, 26; Joes, *Resisting Rebellion*, 135-36.

[89]Krepinevich, *The Army in Vietnam*, 22-24; Spector, *Advice and Assist*, 282-84.

[90]Krepinevich, *The Army in Vietnam*, 25-26; Joes, *Resisting Rebellion*, 135-36.

not flawless, displayed the ARVN's operational potential, while revealing flaws in the overarching defense system. The 7th Division, advised by an American Infantry Lieutenant Colonel, an Infantry Major, and an Intelligence Captain, conducted a multi-regiment limited visibility air assault from American Army and Marine Corps helicopters, far out of range of supporting ground-based artillery, and onto four discrete objectives. Vietnamese National Air Force fighter-bombers flew armed reconnaissance and air-to-ground support. While the scale of the operation is appreciable, there were notable frictions. The enemy departed the area 24 hours prior, leaving only rear-guard forces. ARVN forces captured notable military hardware, to include 81mm mortars and American 50-caliber heavy machine guns, and claimed 131 Vietcong killed, but failure to commit the reserve and close the western egress allowed nearly 300 Vietcong to escape into the darkness.[91] The reason given to the advisor as to why the reserve was not committed was that one regimental commander did not want to share the honor of the victory with another military leader. The American advisors' perceived reality was that the regimental commander who had conducted the majority of the attacks and inflicted the majority of the body count, was better connected in the Diem regime than was the reinforcing commander. The Division commander, who failed to order the reserve into action, was well aware of this, and aware of the glory that Diem would bestow to the reinforcing commander with such a high, second effort body count.[92]

The Advised Forces' Failures

The ARVN and the other nationally resourced military and paramilitary elements failed to pacify the population from the period of 1954 to 1963. This was due to a number of factors,

---

[91]Sheehan, *A Bright and Shining Lie*, 82-89.

[92]Sheehan, *A Bright Shining Lie*, 95-96; Dave Palmer, *Summons of the Trumpet: U.S.-Vietnam in Perspective* (Novato: Presidio Press, 1995), 36-37.

principal among them the effects of the Strategic Hamlet program, the commonplace use of heavy-handed force to control the populace, an American-inspired over-reliance on firepower, and a failure of civil-military relations that began in Saigon and percolated down to the village level. These failures created distance between the legitimate government of South Vietnam and the rural populace, and allowed for a usurpation of the mechanisms of social control by the Vietcong.

Strategic Hamlet

Prime Minister Diem initiated the strategic hamlet system in early 1960. It was modeled from British successes in Malaysia and Philippine successes in the Hukbalahap Rebellion, but it failed in South Vietnam.[93] While the strategic hamlet program was a program innovated at the strategic level, the enforcement and operation of the program fell to the tactical level units.[94] The preponderance of economic influences in the South Vietnam were agrarian production, extracted natural resources for export, and foreign aid based. Like Afghanistan, Vietnam derived most of its state operating costs from foreign aid and investments.[95] There was a gross disparity in wealth between the rural and urban areas—the rural populace largely subsisted on rice and small-hold family farms, and the urban populace thrived on managing trade and services. The rice and other agrarian products also served as currency for the local communist infrastructure, and insurgent fighters that thrived in the south and south-central regions of South Vietnam. The greatest reason for the failure was the ideological disconnection between the Saigon governance and the rural peasants; the peasant attachment to their ancestral lands was a part of their Buddhist religion, and

---

[93]Nagl and Schoomaker, *Learning to Eat Soup with a Knife*, 74-76; Lansdale, *In the Midst of Wars*, 51-54.

[94]Sheehan, *A Bright Shining Lie*, 98-100.

[95]Thomas Barfield, *Afghanistan: A Cultural and Political History* (New Jersey: Princeton University Press, 2010), 315.

31

disrupting the cycles of spirituality, reverence and inheritance doomed the program before it had

an appreciable effect on the insurgency.[96]

Atrocity

Roger Trinquier discusses the relative merits of harsh treatment of a populace, and at

times, selective torture in regards to combatting an insurgency.[97] The ARVN tactical leadership

embraced the practice in dealing with the rural populace, and the Saigon policy makers did

nothing to curtail it, or other atrocities. The ARVN had a propensity to torture as a means for

intelligence gathering. The pervasiveness of the residual Vietminh veterans, the derision that the

ARVN had for the rural populace, and the rise of stealthy and lethal Vietcong attacks developed a

sense of justification in the ARVN leadership's minds. Despite rampant calls against it, and direct

disruption of selected incidents, assigned advisors at the tactical level were unable to halt the

activity without input from higher command echelons.[98]

Over-reliance on Firepower

From 1954 to 1963, the MAAG emphasis on training and development of the ARVN

focused on creating a force that mirrored the United States Army, and was capable of defeating a

multi-axis armored attack from North Vietnam with Chinese support. This was not the force with

which to execute either a counter-insurgent campaign or stability operations, and the emphasis on

the use of firepower displays this. A heavy reliance on indiscriminant force is a poor

counterinsurgency practice, and can often enable the insurgent to use increased animosity among

---

[96]Spector, *Advice and Support*, 332-334; Nagl and Schoomaker, *Learning to Eat Soup with a Knife*, 130-31.

[97]Trinquier, *Modern Warfare*, 44-49.

[98]Sheehan, *A Bright Shining Lie*, 100-106.

the affected population to garner more guns, money and recruits.[99] Several incidents in the

ARVN 7th Division in 1961-62 highlight the predilection to engage with fixed-wing aircraft

against "known VC concentrations, headquarters, storage areas, communications and control

centers, [and] arms manufacturing facilities." When held against the 7th Division's G2

(Intelligence) situational overlay map, these areas matched areas identified as "Viet Cong

hamlets."[100] While there may have been a Viet Cong insurgent presence in these villages,

destroying the village in their entirety through air-to-ground engagement also killed hundreds, if

not thousands, of Buddhist peasants, which further deepened the rift between the populace

outside of Saigon and the ruling elite within the mechanism of the governance.[101] If the

perspective is reframed, and the lessons learned from the positional war with North Korea are

applied to the model of army that the American MAAG created in South Vietnam, then artillery

or air preparatory fires against an objective of uniformed enemy combatants is a perfectly

acceptable tactical mission in which to gain and maintain an advantage of force against a near-

peer opponent. American advisors could not stop each one of these incidents, and the civil and

military leadership in Saigon did not raise objection—the Buddhist populace had little voice with

the central governance to communicate grievance.

Civil-Military Relations

A key friction that hampered the counter-insurgent operations of the ARVN was civil-

military operations. The military establishment, prompted by the Prime Minister, selected and

---

[99]David Kilcullen, *The Accidental Guerrilla: Fighting Small Wars in the Midst of a Big One* (New York: Oxford University Press, 2009), 34-35.

[100]Sheehan, *A Bright Shining Lie*, 113-14.

[101]Sheehan, *A Bright Shining Lie*, 116; Nagl and Schoomaker, *Learning to Eat Soup with a Knife,* 132-33.

promoted officers in the ARVN based on their political reliability, allegiance to Diem, and, to a lesser degree, their Catholicism.[102] It actually became a joke among ARVN officers that promotions and selections were based on the "Three 'D's": *Dang*, Vietnamese for "Party," implying the Can Lao political party; *Dao*, or religion, and; *Du*, which was a reference to Central Vietnam, Diem's home area.[103] The Ministry of Defense recruited private soldiers predominantly from the large urban areas of the small country; as such, they did not have a philosophical connection with the impoverished urban Buddhists, nor did they have residual skills from a youth spent in the jungles or rice paddies.[104] Of village politics, neither the military leaders nor the ARVN soldiers had a firm grasp on what natural village-level political discourse looked like. They could not begin to appreciate the shadow governance that the resurrected Vietcong began emplacing in the heavily populated Mekong Delta region.[105]

Political motivations drove tactical decision-making processes within the ARVN. A risk averse ethos, driven by increasing levels of violence and increased ARVN casualty rates, pervaded Diem and the members of his cabinet. The ARVN 7th Division made a number of mistakes during the Battle of Ap Bac in January 1963 that led to a number of frictions, to include three American helicopters shot down in the opening hour of the battle. The Saigon risk-averse culture manifested by retaining direct control of both Airborne and Mechanized formations, and committing these specialized forces not to complete the encirclement of the VC, but after the threat had dissipated, and the regime-retaining forces (Airborne and Armor) were not at risk.[106]

---

[102]Sheehan, *A Bright Shining Lie*, 205-208; Fall, *The Two Viet-Nams*, 408-09.

[103]Spector, *Advice and Support*, 347.

[104]Sheehan, *A Bright Shining Lie*, 260-263.

[105]Nagl and Schoomaker, *Learning to Eat Soup with a Knife*, 124-25.

[106]Sheehan, *A Bright Shining Lie*, 204-259; Nagl and Schoomaker, *Learning to Eat Soup with a Knife*, 133-34; Palmer, *Summons of the Trumpet*, 25, 38.

Denouement

Several key events in 1963 led to the increased American presence in Vietnam and the transition in roles from combat advisors to combatants. The oppression of the populace by the corrupt Diem regime enabled the political space for the alternate vision—the Vietcong— to grasp a firm foothold among the rural Buddhist populace, and build size and influence by garnering guns, money and recruits. The lack of support for the subnational levels of governance by the Diem regime caused the regime to lose control of the region, save for those areas having the immediate physical presence of ARVN forces. The NLF of the Vietcong filled that vacuum of control. The Battle of Ap Bac raised to American and global consciousness the proficiency of the Vietcong formations, and the inadequacy of the ARVN. The collapse of the Diem regime in November of 1963, and the subsequent cycle of military coups that took faltering control of South Vietnam exasperated the existing frictions of social control of the populace. Lastly, the ARVN had become what the United States military advisors had created them to be—reliant upon roads and aircraft for mobility, quick to send a bullet into an area rather than a soldier, and fixated on defeating a North Korea-like armored thrust at the heart of Saigon. The ARVN also became what the Diem regime wanted them to be. The mid-to-senior level leadership of the ARVN was: politically indebted and subservient to Diem, as opposed to the Office of the Prime Minister; obsessively risk averse, and; focused on maintaining the authority and power of the regime. The compounding nature of these events indicate the demise of the American advisor mission, and set the conditions for President Johnson to commit 44 battalions of American ground combat forces to the Indochina peninsula in July 1965.[107]

---

[107]Nagl and Schoomaker, *Learning to Eat Soup with a Knife*, 153-154.

Analysis

The American advisory effort from 1955-1963 led to the creation of a military that was road bound, uncomfortable in small unit operations, and over-reliant on heavy firepower. While it had the power to control the populace, the operational leaders employed the ARVN in a counter-guerrilla role at best—doing transient, large-scale sweeps of areas, acting upon thin intelligence (or creating it through torture), destroying villages through profligate use of firepower,[108] and then retreating to its bases until the next mission. Lastly, the SVN governmental apparatus viewed the military as predominately a force used to secure the regime and prevent coups—national level leaders in Saigon controlled key assets, such as armored/APC formations, Rangers, airborne and air assault formations. Diem deliberately parsed out such formations to prevent consolidation of power and the potential coup that he feared. In a counter-insurgent struggle, the additional reinforcing capability of such formations is essential to a tactical commander, especially if he knows it is but a radio call away, and under his direct control.[109]

The initial efforts of the American advisor mission failed to identify and target the internally resourced Vietcong insurgency, and left wide gaps in the social control network that enabled the nearly unimpeded growth of the VC. The battle of Ap Bac indicated and demonstrated a rise in the strength, capability and confidence in the largely home-grown rural insurgency of the Vietcong.[110] The increasing corruption, ineffectiveness, and distance of the Diem regime led directly to the military coup of 1 November, and Diem's subsequent execution on 2 November 1963. The failure of the secession of military coup leaderships to reorient the war

---

[108]Sheehan, *A Bright Shining Lie*, 371, 374.

[109]Davidson, *Vietnam at War*, 301-02; Sheehan, *A Bright Shining Lie*, 229-231.

[110]Sheehan, *A Bright Shining Lie*, 113; Nagl and Schoomaker, *Learning to Eat Soup with a Knife*, 133-34.

effort, or even to recognize the ill-suited nature of their own army and situation, added to the social distance between the populace and the governance.[111] The ARVN forces that the Americans built were suited to defeat a North Korean-like penetration offense, but ill designed and led for a COIN campaign. Lastly, but by no means least, the assassination of President Kennedy on 22 November 1963, eliminated the most senior American advocate for a counterinsurgent focus in the RVN.

EL SALVADOR CASE STUDY

> The support of the people is a measure of the insurgents' ability to control the people, whether through their willing cooperation or as the results of threats, acts of terrorism, or the physical occupation of their community. Thus, the insurgent need not possess the hearts and minds of the population, only the minds—the peoples' acquiescence, willing or unwilling, in the revolutionary cause. [112]
>
> —Andrew Krepinevich, 1986

Introduction

American advisor involvement in the El Salvador Civil War was fraught with historic overtures of regional paternalism, containment of communism, and human rights violations. The conflict did not terminate in 1992 with a climatic and triumphal victory over the elements of the insurgency, but a negotiated settlement between the combatants that resulted in fundamental and lasting changes to the infrastructure of the Central American nation-state of El Salvador.[113] While America contributed far more foreign military sales and foreign aid monies than combat elements to assist the Government of El Salvador (GOES), the Spartan advisory effort from both the military and other agencies eventually contributed to the eventual denouement of the conflict, as

---

[111]Davidson, *Vietnam at War*, 297-99.

[112]Krepinevich, *The Army in Vietnam*, 9.

[113]Montgomery, *Revolution in El Salvador*, 9-10, 22.

did the diplomatic efforts from the highest echelons of the American government.[114] Eventually is

the operant word, because similar to the travails experienced by Ramon Magsaysay in the

Philippine Hukbalahap insurrection, nullifying the effects of the insurgency required fundamental

restructuring of the elements of state control of the populace, control and administration of the

coercive powers of the state, and significant social changes within the El Salvador social

construct.[115] The peace settlement and reconciliation that terminated the conflict does offer a

vision of an operational approach for similar conflicts in the future, but the chief risk to mission

success is maintaining the American domestic political will to finish the race. American military

involvement in the El Salvador Civil War spanned four United States presidential terms, but

never attained a level of popular support among the American citizenry.[116]

In relation to McCormick's Model, the GOES initially focused on both Approach 2 and

Approach 3 with the elements of the Armed Forces of El Salvador (ESAF), while attempting,

rather heavy-handedly, to control the population (Approach 1) through ORDEN. The FMLN

controlled rural terrain and populace, and this zero-sum game of balance would have continued

until a side was exhausted, until the GOES changed the rules of the game. Through instituting and

publicizing fundamental changes to liberalize the government and enfranchise the populace, the

GOES denied the FMLN the ideological footholds from which they derived their strength.

The early stages of the Vietnam conflict chiefly dealt with five principal actors, including

the Government of South Vietnam, the ARVN, the Government of North Vietnam, the Vietcong,

and the United States.[117] In contrast, the El Salvador Civil War counted five component groups,

---

[114]Ibid., 177-178.

[115]Lansdale, *In the Midst of Wars*, 45-50, 64-67.

[116]Montgomery, *Revolution in El Salvador*, 21-22.

[117]Palmer, *Summons of the Trumpet*, xx-xxi; Neil Sheehan, *A Bright Shining Lie*, 194-95, 199.

each with distinct agency, in the FMLN alone, which was the principal adversary to the American advisors and GOES. The most influential subgroups in the FMLN included the Popular Forces for Liberation (FPL), and the People's Revolutionary Army (ERP).[118] The military, para-militaries, and various police agencies of El Salvador worked often times at cross-purposes to the government, while a veritable cornucopia of non-governmental actors, to include the Catholic Church and the consortium of affluent landowners, sought to impart their will upon the nation.[119] El Salvador's physical proximity to the United States of America meant that it had experienced hegemonic influences in its past from the North. El Salvador's chief export was coffee beans, a labor-intensive agrarian industry that created conditions of wealth inequality and bourgeois-proletariat confrontations in classic Marxian economic fashion.[120] Physical proximity to other key neighbors, such as Cuba, Honduras, Guatemala, and Nicaragua, enabled influences by both Marxist and Maoist strains of communist revolutionary thought, as well as sanctuary areas, medical treatment, and sources of logistic support. The recently unified Vietnam, ideologically and logistically, also provided support to the FMLN.[121]

---

[118]Danner, *The Massacre at El Mozote*, 21; Wendy Shaull, *Tortillas, Beans, and M-16s: A Year with the Guerrillas in El Salvador* (London: Pluto Press, 1990), 122. The ERP and FPL gained and maintained their influence with both the populace and the policy-makers of the FMLN and FDR through the operation of two clandestine radio networks, Radio Farabundo and Radio Venceremos.

[119]Montgomery, *Revolution in El Salvador*, 86, 155-56.

[120]William Stanley, *The Protection Racket State: Elite Politics, Military Extortion, and Civil War in El Salvador* (Philadelphia, PA: Temple University Press, 1996), 24.

[121]Elisabeth Jean Wood, *Insurgent Collective Action and Civil War in El Salvador* (New York: Cambridge University Press, 2003), 122; Benjamin Schwartz, *American Counterinsurgency Doctrine and El Salvador: The Frustrations of Reform and the Illusions of Nation Building* (Santa Monica: RAND, 1991), 1-2, 8; Bacevich, et al., *American Military Policy in Small Wars*, 6; Max Manwaring and Court Prisk, eds., *El Salvador at War: An Oral History of Conflict from the 1979 Insurrection to the Present* (Washington, DC: National Defense University Press, 1988), 92. Interview with COL John Waghelstein, (MILGRP Commander, 1982-83) reveals both the regional and intercontinental nature of the logistics network that supplied the FMLN.

History of Conflict

The history of the conflict in El Salvador begins with the history of the original conquest and subjugation of the area by the Spanish in 1525. It proceeded through the systematic extermination of the indigenous Amerindian tribes, and culminated in the social and economic domination of the mixed ethnicity peasant class by the aristocratic landowners. Massacre is a part of the national psyche of El Salvador. The very word in Spanish, *matanza,* culturally harkens the Salvadoran to the peasant uprising of 1932 led by Agustin Farabundo Marti, in which paramilitary forces in the services of the wealthy landowners slaughtered an estimated 7,000 to 30,000 peasants, mainly Amerindians.[122] From 1932 until the 1992 peace accords, the military ruled El Salvador with the support of the wealthy coffee plantation owners. Essential to retention of this power was the cooption and empowerment of the mechanisms of coercive state control, namely the military and the police forces. To this end, the wealthy landowners also pooled resources and created the *Organizacion Democratica Nacionalista* (ORDEN), a hyper-conservative paramilitary organization designed to both checkmate rising military power, and to enforce dominion over the peasant class during frequent strikes and attempts for land reform.[123] In the late 1970s, a global recession had as one of its casualties the price of coffee, which plummeted. As the market for coffee beans fell, the primary ripple effect caused real wages in the agrarian-based economy of El Salvador to plummet similarly; secondarily, owners of surplus

---

[122]Philip Russell, *El Salvador in Crisis* (Austin, TX: Colorado River Press, 1984), 37-38; Schwartz, *American Counterinsurgency Doctrine and El Salvador*, 66. Right-leaning militias martyred Agustin Farabundo Marti in 1932 with the Indian peasants, and the FMLN drew their name from him.

[123]Steffen Schmidt, *El Salvador: America's Next Vietnam?* (Salisbury, NC: Documentary Publications, 1983), 63. ORDEN reached a suspected peak strength in 1980 of 80,000 members, and gradually declined through American diplomatic pressures and centrist governmental efforts.

private capital extracted it where possible from El Salvador and reinvested offshore.[124] The resulting civil unrest and violence led a reformist group of ESAF officers to wage a coup against President Romero on 15 October 1979, which served to incite a cascade of violence and an increase in American involvement in El Salvador.[125]

Genesis of American Involvement

America had been involved with the nations of the Caribbean since the earliest days following the American Revolution, but this interaction solidified with the pronouncement of the Monroe Doctrine of 1823, which the Roosevelt Corollary further strengthened in 1904.[126] American business interests have long sought stability in Central America, which encourages both import and export markets. The Monroe doctrine collided with the post-World War II anti-communist Containment Doctrine with the approval of NSC 68 in June 1950.[127] Fidel Castro's communist revolution in nearby Cuba provided a regional springboard for Marxist-inspired, Soviet resourced popular resistance movements in Central and South America, several of which became the precursors and components to the FMLN in El Salvador.[128] Within these strategic contexts, the American government found itself in the inevitable position of stopping communism at its southern border, but trying to execute it without committing American combat forces to an open conflict.

---

[124]Montgomery, *Revolution in El Salvador*, 140-142.

[125]Schmidt, *El Salvador*, 100-101.

[126]Max Boot, *The Savage Wars of Peace: Small Wars and the Rise of American Power* (New York: Basic Books, 2003), 45, 136.

[127]McDougal, *Promised Land, Crusader State*, 165.

[128]Montgomery, *Revolution in El Salvador*, 116-118

While the Salvadoran Ambassadorial military group was in existence for years, it received a tremendous influx of capital and talent to effect the direction of the stricken country following the coup. Unlike the adversarial nature of the American Department of State and Department of Defense efforts in Vietnam, the U.S. Ambassador eventually directed the conduct of the counterinsurgent campaign in cooperation with United States Southern Command (USSOUTHCOM) and the Military Group (MILGRP) commanders. Early stages of this relationship had a level of friction, which slowed the advisorship efforts at the secretarial and subnational levels.[129] Early in 1981, American diplomatic and military leaders begin discussing the root causes of the insurgency with their El Salvadoran counterparts and, surprisingly, found mutual accord. Attaining the desired state of relative peace would require wholesale shifts in the social, economic, and security mechanisms of the small nation. The decision makers in El Salvador were loath to institute such changes, as they would compromise their own positions of relative power.[130]

Evolution of American Involvement

American involvement in the El Salvadoran Civil War was slow and relatively ineffectual, at first. A number of restraints stood in the path of the SOUTHCOM commander, not the least were public and international perspectives on human rights abuses by the GOES, a

---

[129]Manwaring and Prisk, eds., *El Salvador at War*, 100-106. Interviews with GEN Wallace Nutting (USSOUTHCOM Commander, 1979-83), Ambassador Deane Hinton (U.S. Ambassador to El Salvador, 1982-1983), and COL John Waghelstein (MILGRP Commander, 1982-3).

[130]Bacevich, et al., *American Military Policy in Small Wars*, 6; Schwartz, *American Counterinsurgency Doctrine and El Salvador*, 62-64.

highly politicized and fractured GOES, and American anti-war sentiment encapsulated in the phrase "Vietnam Syndrome."[131]

Both sides of the El Salvador political spectrum participated in atrocity, either the right-wing sponsored repression of the peasant class on behalf of the wealthy landowners, or the left-wing assassinations and targeting of mid-to-senior level social, political, military and business leadership. This was manifest in the events surrounding the Miss Universe Pageant Massacre in July of 1975. As the GOES attempted to develop El Salvador as a tourist attraction and bring international income to the country, the event on 19 July inspired Leftist demonstrations against the military government and the social injustice propagated by the landowners. The riots led to harsh crackdowns by the paramilitary ORDEN and state security agencies; the right wing and governance killed 12 students, and the international press was there to cover the event.[132]

The GOES and ESAF nested together with a history of economic class violence and social caste structure. Military officers attended the solitary military academy in El Salvador, and this shared experience bound them together in a *tanda,* which is a word to describe the graduating class of any given year, but implies fraternal bonds and a leadership hierarchy that supersedes the existing military justice system, or the pressures exerted by civilian authorities. Officers, commonly the scions of the wealthy landowners, or generational military members, used the *tanda* system to advance their own careers, exert patronage to upcoming leaders, and to create dense webs of protection for themselves.[133] In 1979, the military forces of El Salvador were very rudimentary in structure, sophistication, and professionalization, and lacked a strong civil-

---

[131]Schmidt, *El Salvador,* 124; Schwartz, *American Counterinsurgency Doctrine and El Salvador,* 12.

[132]Schmidt, *El Salvador,* 86; Russell, *El Salvador in Crisis,* 129-30.

[133]Schwartz, *American Counterinsurgency Doctrine and El Salvador,* 18-19; Montgomery, *Revolution in El Salvador,* 38-9.

military relationship because the elite officer corps of the military *was* the leadership of the state.[134] Graft, corruption and self-aggrandizement were the metrics of personal success for an officer, and a downtrodden peasant population seeking social revolution from the affluent landowner class sustained a semi-permanent state of crisis that enabled the military to stay in power. Every so many years, a senior officer in his colonelcy would secure the support of enough of his *tanda* class, and would wage a bloody (or bloodless) coup to seize control of the civil governance, often replacing the older colonel or general that had executed the same usurpation two to three years prior.[135]

The "Vietnam Syndrome" was but one facet of the conflict that placed constraints on the American advisor team in El Salvador, but America's recent history in Vietnam framed the strategic environment wherein the United States found itself. Both Presidents Carter and Reagan faced a number of strategic and regional crises in the late 1970s and early 1980s: the Iran hostage situation; the Desert One rescue attempt in Iran; the Soviet invasion of Afghanistan; communist insurgencies and governments in Cuba, Honduras, Dominican Republic, Mexico, Columbia, and Nicaragua; Communist overtures toward Angola, Ethiopia, Cambodia, and Laos, and; firebombing of American embassies in Libya and Pakistan.[136] These crises pushed the boundaries of either NSC 68 (containment strategy) or the Monroe Doctrine/Roosevelt Corollary, or both. In light of all of these pressures, placing American combat boots on the ground was still a viable option, even through the Vietnam War only terminated seven years prior, creating so much

---

[134]Stanley, *The Protection Racket State*, 26-7; Bacevich, et al., *American Military Policy in Small Wars*, 14.

[135]Montgomery, *Revolution in El Salvador*, 165.

[136]Schmidt, *El Salvador*, 15-16, 89; Bacevich, et al., *American Military Policy in Small Wars*, 3-4.

domestic strife, political upheaval, and furor.[137] Whereas the FMLN retained a fear of direct

combat intervention by regular American forces,[138] the U.S. domestic political environment

would not support a large ground force, and barely supported the efforts undertaken by the

MILGRP in light of the rampant atrocities in El Salvador.[139] Despite these pressures, the first

three Operations, Plans and Training Teams (OPATT) deployed to El Salvador on 14 January

1980, and began working at the ESAF infantry brigade echelons.[140]

The Advised Element

The military effort in El Salvador represented one of the four instruments of national

power (Diplomatic, Informational, Military and Economic, or DIME). Like the MAAG in

Vietnam, the MILGRP was subordinate to the Ambassador, and the geographic combatant

commander.[141] Unlike Vietnam, the United States foreign policy restrained the MILGRP in El

Salvador insofar as mission scope and strength. This necessitated an overarching operational

approach that relied more heavily on the Diplomatic, Informational and Economic elements of

DIME. As such, the American strategic outlook eventually raised the scope of the MILGRP

above the tactical level Army formations, focused more heavily on the Corps and higher echelons

of staff, and the training and professionalization of the officer and non-commissioned officer

---

[137]Lind, *Vietnam: The Necessary War*, 269-71; Schmidt, *El Salvador*, 129. Known infamously as "Reagan's 55," the number of advisors authorized in the MILGRP was not to exceed a boots on the ground strength greater than 55, nor where they authorized to conduct combat operations with the ESAF. These controls slackened in the late-1980s, but strength never exceeded 150 American service people.

[138]Shaull, *Tortillas, Beans, and M-16s: a Year with the Guerrillas in El Salvador,* 36, 49.

[139]Schmidt, *El Salvador*, 19-20.

[140]Schwartz, *American Counterinsurgent Doctrine and El Salvador*, 87; Bacevich, et al., *American Military Policy in Small Wars*, 17.

[141]Chairman, Joint Chiefs of Staff, JP 5.0, *Joint Operations Planning*, IV-13.

corp.[142] Utilizing a "whole of government" approach, the advisors and the Ambassadorial staff affected positive change in the El Salvador military establishment. Due to the thin walls between senior military leadership and the political leadership, changes made to the Army changed attitudes and actions of the government.[143]

The Advised Successes

As a counterinsurgent effort, the combination of effects by the political leadership of El Salvador to liberalize the political space nested well with the effects of modernizing and professionalizing the military elements of the GOES. There was a learning curve in the period of conflict, though. In 1979, the ESAF was rudimentarily structured, ill-equipped and led, installation bound, and highly corrupt. Vast expanses of rural El Salvador were in the throes of insurgent activity, and the central government was struggling to maintain control through its intermediaries and the municipal level.

Force Development

The Armed Forces of El Salvador, with American monies and advisorship, expanded from an *ex ante* strength of 11,000 to a strength of 56,000 by 1988. The armed forces of the GOES included the Air Force, Army, Navy, the National Police, the Treasury Police, and the National Guard.[144] American money was key to influencing political actions at the highest echelons, and to keeping the military machine of the ESAF working. One intermediate goal in 1984 was to create and outfit 39 light infantry battalions, one engineering battalion, and two quick reaction battalions, along with the required rotary-wing lift and attack assets, fixed wing

---

[142]Schwartz, *American Counterinsurgent Doctrine and El Salvador*, 8-9, 11.

[143]Ibid., 25-26.

[144]Schwarz, *American Counterinsurgency Doctrine and El Salvador*, 2-3;

fighter-bombers, and fixed wing lift assets.[145] From a relative pittance in 1979 of $3.5 million per annum,[146] the United States was financing both the GOES and the El Salvador military to the tune of $1-1.5 million a day in 1988.[147] By 1990, the United States invested a total of $6 billion into defeating the FMLN insurgency in El Salvador, and the conflict had two more years until the combatants signed a peace accord.[148]

Significant to this force structure and the prevalent military culture was the existence of only one military academy—all officers of all the services graduated with strong fraternal bonds that created ties between members of the same year group. These ties breached the normal organizational boundaries of what, in America, would be nearly impenetrable walls of inter-service rivalry and patriarchy. The *tanda* system, or graduating-class "protection association," created the political room to consolidate internal coercive force and served as an extra-regulatory means of control of the ESAF. The *tanda* system enabled the rampant corruption prevalent in the officer ranks, such as collecting the pay of 'ghost enlistees' (non-existing soldiers carried on the payrolls), or siphoning American assistance dollars off to private interests.[149] As MILGRP approached the problem of professionalization in 1980, it represented the first institutional frictions they had to address at the tactical, operational and strategic levels, given the history of

---

[145]Stanley, *The Protection Racket State*, 228.

[146]Stephanie Neuman, *Military Assistance in Recent Wars: the Dominance of the Superpowers* (Washington, DC: Praeger Publishers, 1987), 14.

[147]Montgomery, *Revolution in El Salvador*, 21.

[148]Schwarz, *American Counterinsurgency Doctrine and El Salvador*, v.

[149]R.A. Rail, *El Salvador Advisor: Toward a Military Personnel Advisory Doctrine* (Kansas City, MO: Ragal Limited Editions, 1992), 30-31; Schwartz, *American Counterinsurgency Doctrine and El Salvador*, 19.

military governance of the civil domain.[150] This is a significant temporal diametric, because during the same period in time, the FMLN expanded their operations to all fourteen provinces of the small country.[151]

Professionalization Efforts

The MILGRP leadership saw that a key to influencing the liberalization of the central governance of El Salvador was to enhance the liberalization, and professionalization, of the elements of the ESAF that had the most contact with the populace.[152] The MILGRP attempted this daunting task via a number of approaches, and was only partially effective when an observer regards the results along a singular line of effort.

The American advisors reached back to the Army's experiences with the MAAG and the ARVN in the early stages of Vietnam for inspiration, but also attempted something new in their approaches to developing the Salvadoran Army. Attempting to decrease the influence of the *tanda* network over time, OPATTs, through the Embassy and MILGRP, enrolled Salvadoran officers in the U.S. Army Infantry Officer Basic and Advanced Courses in Fort Benning, Georgia, and the U.S. Army Command and General Staff College in Fort Leavenworth, Kansas.[153] The non-commissioned officer corps in the ESAF was nearly non-existent; advisors, mostly senior U.S. Army Special Forces non-commissioned officers, established NCO academies in San Salvador, the national capital. NCOs could also attend the School of the Americas in the Panama

---

[150]Bacevich, et al., *American Military Policy in Small Wars*, 26-27; Schwartz, *American Counterinsurgency Doctrine and El Salvador*, 18-19.

[151]Montgomery, *Revolution in El Salvador*, 21.

[152]Schwartz, *American Counterinsurgency Doctrine and El Salvador*, vi-vii. Derived from the Kissinger Commission Report of 1984, the MILGRP operational approach solidified around three Lines of Effort (LOE): reform ESAF; land reform and redistribution, and; democratization.

[153]Montgomery, *Revolution in El Salvador*, 167; Bacevich, et al., *American Military Policy in Small Wars*, 15.

Canal Zone, Panama, and American NCO schools in the Continental United States.[154] Foreign Military Sales, through the American embassy, provided the latest in American light and medium weaponry and equipment, to include M16A1 rifles, M203 grenade launchers, M60 medium machine guns, FM radios, night vision devises, light and medium mortars, and 105mm artillery, complete with all required ammunition, batteries, and maintenance plans.[155] Lastly, but most innovatively, entire ESAF battalion formations were extricated from the conflict to Panama, Fort Bragg, North Carolina, or Fort Benning, Georgia, for in-depth immersion training in light infantry and counterinsurgent tactics. Most notable of these was the Belloso Battalion, which was the first to receive training in Fort Bragg in January 1982.[156]

Civil-Military Political Realignment

<u>Depowering the Military at the Policy Level</u>

Then Vice President Bush personally visited El Salvador to communicate President Reagan's personal interest in the freedom and transparency of the upcoming Presidential elections, and the President's concerns over the right-wing death squads' activities, particularly their co-membership in the armed forces of El Salvador. Reagan tied his interest to the flow of American money. The elections were subsequently open and free, and with a 54 percent majority, the populace elected Napoleon Duarte from the centrist *Partido Democrata Christiano*

---

[154]Bacevich, et al., *American Military Policy in Small Wars*, 27-28.

[155]Shaull, *Tortillas, Beans and M16s*, 55-56; Danner, *The Massacre at El Mozote*, 49-50, 52.

[156]Montgomery, *Revolution in El Salvador*, 152; Manwaring and Prisk, eds., *El Salvador at War*, 235-237, interview with COL John Waghelstein (MILGRP Commander, 1982-3).

(PDC) Christian Democrat party.[157] This is significant, because Duarte beat out the right-wing military heir-apparent of the *Alianza Republicana Nacionalista* (ARENA) party, Roberto D'Aubuisson, a former intelligence officer who was earlier arrested for the 1980 murder of Archbishop Roberto Romero in March of 1980.[158] Also significant was the successful turnout to the polls, regardless of party affiliation. Though not at the rates of the 1982 elections, FMLN violence had peaked in the weeks prior to the election, and the Communist narrative was that any vote for either party warranted death for the voter. A counterpoint is required for these seemingly positive violence assessments. In 1982, 28 municipalities did not vote in the presidential elections, as the physical terrain and populace was under the direct control of the FMLN. In 1984, 58 municipalities did not vote, for the same reason.[159]

Political Liberalism

Military governments ran El Salvador since 1948, arriving in power following a coup. Competing *juntas* waged a war of narrative, claiming to be more progressive and more revolutionary than their predecessors, but always falling back into the normal models of control that involved violent repression of the underclass, and continuing the cult of corruption enabled by the *tanda* system. As the military *juntas* attempted to serve their two masters (the *tanda*

---

[157]Montgomery, *Revolution in El Salvador*, 177-178; Schwartz, *American Counterinsurgency Doctrine and El Salvador*, 10, 88. Reagan's specificities describe what a modern planner would recognize as Lines of Effort (LOE) from a non-terrain based Operational Approach for Wide Area Security from JP 5.0: Democracy, Development, Dialogue, and Defense.

[158]Russell, *El Salvador in Crisis*, 90, 96. Interestingly, the judge assigned to review D'Aubuisson's case was a *tanda*-mate of D'Aubuisson. The judge dismissed the case for lack of evidence, but D'Aubuisson was one of the named ESAF officers that Vice President George H.W. Bush demanded be investigated for Romero's murder, among many other atrocities associated with ORDEN activities.

[159]Russell, *El Salvador in Crisis*, 96-97.

system and the wealthy landowners), the mechanisms of control of the government progressively lost their tenacity, forcing the government ever more into use of the only reliable form of control – directed political violence.[160]

As the civil war increased in ferocity after the Duarte inauguration in 1984, the military leadership waned in political preeminence under American diplomatic and military influence. As power gradually shifted back to civilian control, the various competing political parties had also to fight a war for political legitimacy, between both themselves, and the *Frente Democratico Revolucionario* (FDR), which was the political arm of the FMLN. Duarte, receiving coaching from both the U.S. Ambassadorial Staff and other mentors within the U.S. Congress, recognized that the conflict must end, or at least taper within the strategic setting of the remainder of American foreign policy interests. Duarte took an initial step, and called for a meeting between himself, the FMLN and the FDR on 15 October 1984, in the small town of La Palma, Chalatenango Province. While this meeting, and a subsequent one in November would be the last between the constitutional governance and the insurgency representatives for nearly three years, contemporary politicians and diplomats from Central and North America foresaw these initial meetings as the seed that would eventually bring forth the peace accords in 1992.[161]

Joint Operations Conducted By ESAF

The ESAF eventually worked to a level of proficiency at large scale combined arms operations. As in Vietnam, and similar to both the ARVN and subsequent American formations, the ESAF massed their firepower and coercive potential and controlled the area that they were deployed to. Moreover, similar to Vietnam, when the ESAF terminated the large-scale operation

---

[160]Schmidt, *El Salvador*, 89; Stanley, *The Protection Racket State*, 168-169.

[161]Montgomery, *Revolution in El Salvador*, 187-189; Stanley, *The Protection Racket State*, 33.

and the security force returned to its sprawling bases in the urban center of the country, the insurgent force reconstituted and reclaimed its authority in the rural villages and municipalities.[162] As the war proceeded through the 1980s and ESAF professionalism and proficiency increased, the security forces were increasingly capable of conducting smaller scale, longer duration operations commensurate with counterinsurgent best practices.[163]

In the war of ideas, and in an attempt to regain political space, the ESAF dedicated considerable effort to eliminating the Radio Farabundo and Radio Venceremos information network through offensive action.[164] The mission to eliminate the influence of the Venceremos radio network ultimately became the life work of COL Domingo Monteressa and the infamous Atlacatl Battalion.[165] Operations in El Mozote (1981), Tamarindo (1984), and Morazan (1984) hampered both radio operations and the spread of FMLN propaganda for limited periods.[166] As with the predominance of large-scale, short duration ESAF operations, the radio station re-emerged into the soon-abandoned space, and continued to serve as the voice of the FDR shadow governance of the rural areas. The sub-objective of capture or destroy the radio stations was not realized in these operations, but the large scale sweeps disrupted the FMLN operations, destroyed or captured arms caches, and challenged the insurgent control of the contested rural space. The

---

[162]Shaull, *Tortillas, Beans and M16s,*

[163]Galula, *Counterinsurgency Warfare,* 65.

[164]Shaull, *Tortillas, Beans, and M-16s,* 33, 56.

[165]Danner, *Massacre at El Mozote,* 149-154. Monteressa was killed on 22 October 1984 after capturing what he thought was the elusive transmitter for Radio Venceremos. In reality, it was a command-detonated improvised explosive device, and insurgents blew his helicopter out of the sky as he was returning to San Salvador with his "trophy". Monteressa's remains fell near the destroyed village of El Mozote, a rural town wherein his Atlacatl Battalion slaughtered 800 men, women and children in December 1981.

[166]Danner, *Massacre at El Mozote,* 22-24; Shaull, *Tortillas, Beans, and M16s,* 76-78; the Tamarindo operation also involved the equally famed Belloso Battalion, the first ESAF unit extracted from the fight, trained in Fort Bragg, and returned to El Salvador; Montgomery, *Revolution in El Salvador,* 151-2.

synchronizing capacity and joint ability of the ESAF further demonstrated the political message

of the vastly improved unity of purpose of the ESAF, much to the FMLN chagrin.[167]

The Advised Failures

Noted earlier, El Salvador organized their political environment of coercion and control

around maintaining the power base of the wealthy landowners over the massed peasant

population. In the decades leading to the 1979 coup and subsequent civil war, discriminant

violence the technique GOES, ORDEN, and ESAF used purposefully to prevent popular uprising

or power-sharing initiatives. The GOES and ESAF continued these practices in the early stages of

the Civil War, and further fueled the insurgency until such activities declined.

Atrocity

A salient theme of the El Salvador Civil War was the use of atrocity by either side of the

conflict to both control the population, and attempt attrition of the opponent. The atrocities waged

upon the populace by both ESAF and ORDEN created additional frictions for the MILGRP

advisors, the U.S. Ambassadorial staff, and the American political leadership.

Right-wing Extrajudicial Actions

The chief problem facing the succession of progressive *juntas* from 1979 was the friction

between the populace' expectation of proactive measures against the right-wing paramilitaries,

and actual execution of the disbanding of the paramilitaries. An approach that solidified through

the years was for the central governance to cede that information operation to the political left,

---

[167]Manwaring and Prisk, eds., *El Salvador at War*, 92, 277-278, 295-296; interviews with COL John Waghelstein (MILGRP Commander, 1982-3), *Comandante* Miguel Castrollanos (Insurgent Leader, 1973-85), and COL Rene Emilio Ponce (C3 (Operations Officer), ESAF Combined Staff).

represented by the peasants and labor union.[168] While this approach eventually led to the 1991-92 reconciliation between the political left and right wings, it had at its genesis the dissolution of the ORDEN as the fulfillment of a *junta* political plank.[169]

The ORDEN served an early function as the enforcement arm of the landowners against the peasants and the unions.[170] They targeted religious leaders that espoused liberation theology, union leadership, small business owners, and left-of-center petty bureaucrats within the sub-national governance. Victims were commonly beheaded or otherwise mutilated, and left in public spaces purposefully to be found, or were specifically "disappeared," the only statement made by the very disappearance of someone involved in an activity that was contrary to the ruling party or power.[171] Within this capacity, they were moderately successful, but also created new insurgents through their prolific use of atrocity, terrorism, and murder.[172] One author compares their murderous actions against political opponents as reminiscent of the CIA-led Phoenix program in the Vietnam conflict.[173] As the 1980s progressed, and the flow of American aid monies became more dependent on the reduction of atrocity, ORDEN decreased in size, but became part of the political machine of the ARENA party. It was in this capacity that the ORDEN canvassed the

---

[168]Schmidt, *El Salvador*, 109.

[169]Ibid., 92.

[170]Stanley, *The Protection Racket State*, 27.

[171]Schmidt, *El Salvador*, 63-65, 88; Russell, *El Salvador in Crisis*, 134-135. The prevalent tactic of making a political target completely vanish became so prevalent that "disappeared" entered the El Salvadoran vernacular as a double past tense verb, e.g. "Their whole family was disappeared last night".

[172]Gordon McCormick and Frank Giordano, "Things Come Together: Symbolic Violence and Guerrilla Mobilisation," *Third World Quarterly* 28, no. 2 (2007): 295-332, http://www.tandfonline.com/doi/abs/10.1080/01436590601153705#.U0mxoO9OXX4 (accessed 12 April 2014), 299; Kilcullen, *The Accidental Guerrilla*, 35.

[173]Russell, *El Salvador in Crisis*, 120.

available breadth and depth of the country in support of the ARENA party and D'Aubuisson in the 1984 electoral cycle.[174]

ESAF Atrocity and Targeting of Civilian Populations

In reaction to the FMLN strategy of long duration people's war, the ESAF initially adopted a counter-strategy of removing the fish (insurgent) from the sea (populace) by drying up the sea.[175] Example massacres in El Mozote (1981), Tamarindo (1984), and Morazan (1984), Los Vueltas, and Los Llanitos (1984)[176] were derivatives of this initial strategy as the GOES and ESAF struck back blindly against what they presumed were FMLN haven areas. The ESAF used large hammer and anvil tactics that would have been recognizable to any Vietnam veteran from 1960-1970, and made wide use of indiscriminant indirect and fixed wing fire support.[177] While the early operations were horrible at surface value, the negative strategic value of atrocity continued to plague the GOES and ESAF through the remainder of the civil war, and played a large influence in the international efforts to terminate the conflict with a power-sharing accord oriented on a centrist governance. The reports of the slaughter of thousands of perceived innocents horrified the American populace and international human rights watchers. Through their elected representatives, the people indicated a decline in popular will to support a corrupt

---

[174]Ibid., 92-93.

[175]Danner, *Massacre at El Mozote*, 141.

[176]Danner, *Massacre at El Mozote*, 22-24; Shaull, *Tortillas, Beans, and M16s*, 76-78; Montgomery, *Revolution in El Salvador*, 151-152; Schwartz, *American Counterinsurgency Doctrine and El Salvador*, 87.

[177]Montgomery, *Revolution in El Salvador*, 150-152; Schwartz, *American Counterinsurgency Doctrine and El Salvador*, 3, 17, 31, 36.

Latin American government, which placed additional friction in the path of President Reagan, USSOUTHCOM Commander, and the MILGRP Commander.[178]

Denouement

In 1989, the guerrillas and the governance fought each other to a stalemate, with no tactical actions shaping the environment until FMLN representatives and GOES President Cristiani signed the peace accords in Mexico City on 16 January 1992.[179] The FMLN could not mass and deliver a resounding defeat to the central core of the GOES power base, either in San Salvador, or against the powerful ESAF. The ESAF, and by extension, the GOES, could not deny the FMLN of the rural population support, prevent military and civil servant defections to the FMLN, nor secure for themselves the active support from the rural or urban populace that connoted success along Approach 2 of McCormick's Diamond. Both combatant elements had shifted their tactics throughout the decade, waxing and waning both from small-scale stability operations to battalion-sized or larger deliberate attacks.[180]

Analysis

Though not clean and quick, the reformation of the political system created better conditions for conflict termination than did the military approaches. Reforming the military increased their capacity and capability to prevent the communist FMLN from outright overrunning the seat of government in San Salvador (McCormick's Approach 1), thusly creating the political maneuver room for a gradual liberalization of the governments mechanisms. The challenge was never to eliminate every political adversary, labor union leader, liberation theology

---

[178]Montgomery, *Revolution in El Salvador*, 171-172.

[179]Ibid., 224-225.

[180]Schwartz, *American Counterinsurgency Doctrine and El Salvador*, 17.

priest, or FMLN guerrilla, but it was to make good on the reformist promises that the FMLN and

FDR made to the populace.

ANALYSIS AND CONCLUSION

> Learn all you can.... Get to know their families, clans and tribes, friends and enemies, wells, hills and roads. Do all this by listening and by indirect inquiry. ... Get to speak their dialect ... not yours. Until you can understand their allusions, avoid getting deep into conversation or you will drop bricks. [181]
>
> —T.E. Lawrence, 1917

Analyzing El Salvador and Vietnam from a counterinsurgent perspective, especially

when filtered through the McCormick Model, reveals some interesting correlations between the

effectiveness of a governmental counterinsurgent force, and the echelon of a host governance that

U.S. advisory forces placed the most emphasis on. There is a correlation that can be drawn from

the research: the higher the echelon in a host country that can be influenced, the more success the

overall counterinsurgent effort has. A caveat, however – the most suitable advisor for a cabinet

minister or secretary-level position or a military Chief of Staff may not be a U.S. serviceperson.

In addition to the Department of State representatives attached to the Embassy, advisorship and

influence ought to come from the totality of JIIM elements, and should maintain a balance among

the DIME instruments of national power. If the population is the Clausewitzian center of gravity

in a counterinsurgent fight or wide area security operation, all instruments of national power

should be oriented toward securing that center of gravity, by both direct and indirect means. El

Salvadoran political leaders took an indirect route to securing the population by instilling

governmental reform and addressing the popular grievances. South Vietnam leadership

exacerbated the popular grievances and further marginalized the population, directly enabling the

Vietcong insurgency to grow large enough to require infusion of exogenous security forces.

---

[181]T. E. Lawrence, "27 Articles," *TE Lawrence Studies,* http://www.telstudies.org/ writings/works/articles_essays/1917_twenty-seven_articles.shtml (access 21 February 2014).

During the Vietnam advisory period of 1955-1963, the American operational leadership placed emphasis on creating a near-mirror image of the American Army as it stood in the aftermath of the Korean conflict of 1950-53. Given recent history, they believed the likely North Vietnam course of action would replicate the North Korean armored thrust into South Korea, and prepared the ARVN to counter that threat. Neither the embassy nor the MAAG respected the power of the long duration peoples' war that Ho Chi Minh had launched in South Vietnam with the remnants of the Vietminh. While ARVN battalions and other security forces abused and oppressed the Buddhist rural population and fought tactically insignificant battles with shards of Vietcong units, the National Liberation Front was clandestinely moving through the villages and strategic hamlets, steadily acquiring guns, recruits, and money in a zero-sum game for population control. Relative to McCormick's diamond, the ARVN and the Saigon governance focused too heavily on pursuing Approach 2 (Target the Intermediate Agents) and Approach 3 (Target the Strategic Apex) with its heavy-handed techniques, while ignoring Approach 3 (Control the Population), an oversight that allowed the Vietcong insurgency to seize that political and physical terrain, and blossom in size beyond control.

At the onset of America's involvement of the El Salvadoran Civil War, the operational planners more accurately determined the nature of the complex problem that they faced. One most pressing was the shadow of Vietnam looming over them, and secondarily an American popular sentiment that could not stomach perceptions of mass support for the rampant corruption in El Salvador. These contextual issues placed restraint on U.S. support of the GOES. Fortunately, the mental agility of both the U.S. Ambassadorial staff, USSOUTHCOM and MILGRP recognized the growth potentiality of a rural people's war, and focused their efforts on addressing the inciting conditions for the social instability. While the United States spent quite a considerable sum on modernizing and professionalizing the ESAF, the JIIM advisor elements placed their decisive effort on reformation of the central governance; trickle down liberalism percolated to the local governance and security forces. In relation to McCormick's Model of analysis, the GOES initially focused on both Approach 2 and Approach 3 with the elements of the ESAF, while attempting, rather heavy-handedly, to control the population (Approach 1) through ORDEN. The FMLN controlled rural terrain and populace, and this zero-sum game of balance would have continued until a side was exhausted, until the GOES changed the rules of the game. Through instituting and publicizing fundamental changes to liberalize the government and enfranchise the populace, the GOES denied the FMLN the ideological footholds from which they derived their strength.

Our contemporary doctrine, Unified Land Operations, remarks upon and requires extensive use of JIIM operations to execute our current United States strategic policies.[182] While history does not repeat itself, it occasionally rhymes with events more contemporary. An astute observer can see modern parallels to the events of 1955-63 and 1979-92 in three of the theaters in our current Global War on Terror (GWOT)-originated Overseas Contingency Operations (OCO). These include Afghanistan (Operation Enduring Freedom (OEF), the Philippines (OEF-P), and in the recently concluded Operation Iraqi Freedom (OIF).

Application

This case study contributes to the continuum of asymmetric warfare knowledge that has existed since Sun Tzu, but focusses on analyzing and creating operational approaches available to present day American and like-minded militaries fighting within a JIIM environment. [183] Low-intensity conflict, limited objectives, stability operations and counterinsurgent efforts represent the highest likelihood of the spectrum of conflict American military will be committed to for the

---

[182]ADP 3-0, *Unified Land Operations,* 1-3—1-6.

[183]Sun Tzu, *The Art of War*, trans. Samuel B. Griffith (New York: Oxford University Press, 1963), 76.

near future.[184] This provides those future operational level planners a historical insight into successful and unsuccessful approaches, and their effects. Lastly, this study validates the concept of the McCormick Model when applied to a comparative case study. To fully realize the potential of the model, further research could use it in conjunction with a "large N" study as a final arbiter of operationalized data points. A serious effort, encapsulating 20-30 individual low-intensity conflicts from multiple regions of the world, and with multiple nationalities as protagonist or antagonist, would advance the existing knowledge base on mapping and possibly predicting growth rates and expanse of insurgent forces.

As an example, consider the following trio of data points in a given time period in a given conflict from a situational awareness and a predictive analysis perspective. In 1953, and when working with nationalist Vietnamese in the government tax collection agency in Hanoi, Bernard Fall determined that the bulk of a so-called pacified region of 8000 villages in the Red River Delta had ceased paying taxes to the central government. Tax collection being a premise of governmental control of a population, and exists in the McCormick Model as Approach 2. Another hypothesis that he tested was the presence or absence of government assigned or appointed teachers in the region, assuming that no teachers in an area that was not paying taxes was a good indicator of Communist control of the population. Events later proved Fall accurate, as the entire area, claimed to be under French military control, collapsed in front of Communist formations after the Battle of Dien Bien Phu in May 1954.[185] While these data points indicate a *fait accompli* of communist control, from 1957 to 1959, Fall analyzed the assassination patterns

---

[184]Gian Gentile, "Let's Build an Army to Win All Wars," *Joint Forces Quarterly* 52 (1st Quarter 2009): 27–33, http://www.thefreelibrary.com/Let's+build+an+army+to+win+all+wars.-a0193510865 (accessed 13 October 2010); John Nagl, "Let's Win the Wars We're In," *Joint Forces Quarterly* 52, 1st Quarter (2009): 20-26, http://www.au.af.mil/au/awc/awcgate/jfq/nagl_win_wars.pdf (accessed 13 October 2010).

[185]Fall, *The Two Viet-Nams*, 51-52.

of village chieftains (sub-national civil leadership, Approach 2) in South Vietnam, determining that by 1960, "...the communists had killed about 10,000 village chiefs in a country that has 16,000 villages."[186] These deaths began in the mid-1950s, and clearly indicator a contestation for the control of an affected population.

Unanswered Questions

The hypothesis that frugal application of military power, and directed mentorship and development efforts at the subnational and national level of a targeted governance, has a great level of validity in this present era of fiscal restraint and war weariness. The judicious use of non-military elements of national power in El Salvador may have prevented a US Military presence in operational numbers, but where there hidden costs? Vietnam was clearly a battle fought within the larger context of the Cold War between the United States and the Soviet Bloc, but the early stages operated in the shadow of the Korean War.[187] In applying similar containment policy to El Salvador, was there a cognition on the part of the National Security mechanisms of a terminus point of the Cold War, and thusly a lack of clear and present danger? The so-called "Vietnam Syndrome" did affect our national leaders during the decision cycles to commit national effort in El Salvador.[188] Have the last 13 years of conflict created an Afghanistan or Iraq Syndrome that will affect our national decision making authorities in the coming decades, and will we be able to leap cognitively past that bias and approach unique problem sets unencumbered? Time will tell.

---

[186]Ibid., 52-53.

[187]Lind, *Vietnam: The Necessary War*, 265-266, 269.

[188]Mark Danner, *The Massacre at El Mozote: a Parable of the Cold War*, 40-42.

BIBLIOGRAPHY

Bacevich, Andrew, James Hallums, Richard White, and Thomas Young. *American Military Policy in Small Wars: The Case of El Salvador*. Washington: Pergamon-Brassey's, 1988.

Barfield, Thomas. *Afghanistan: A Cultural and Political History*. New Jersey: Princeton University Press, 2010.

Boot, Max. *The Savage Wars of Peace: Small Wars and the Rise of American Power*. New York: Basic Books, 2003.

Clausewitz, Carl von. *On War*. Translated by Michael Eliot Howard and Peter Paret. Reprint. Princeton: Princeton University Press, 1989.

Coll, Steve. *Ghost Wars: The Secret History of the CIA, Afghanistan and Bin Laden From the Soviet Invasion to September 10, 2001*. New York: Penguin, 2004.

Cosmas, Graham. *MACV: The Joint Command in the Years of Escalation 1962-1967*. Washington, DC: Government Printing Office, 2006.

Danner, Mark. *The Massacre at El Mozote: A Parable of the Cold War*. New York: Vintage, 1994.

Davidson, Philip. *Vietnam at War: The History 1946-1975*. New York, Oxford University Press, 1991.

Engdahl, F. William. "The War in Mali and AFRICOM's Agenda: Target China." *Global Research*. http://www.globalresearch.ca/the-war-in-mali-and-africoms-african-agenda-target-china/5322517 (accessed 15 February 2014).

Fall, Bernard B. *The Two Viet-Nams: A Political and Military Analysis*. 2nd ed. Washington, DC: Frederick A. Praeger Publishers, 1967.

Freedom House. "El Salvador." Freedom in the World. http://www.freedomhouse.org/report/freedom-world/2013/el-salvador#.U0ritO9OXX4 (accessed 13 March 2014).

_____. "Vietnam." Freedom in the World. http://www.freedomhouse.org/report/ freedom-world/2013/vietnam#.U0rkuO9OXX4 (accessed 13 March 2014).

Galula, David. *Counterinsurgency Warfare: Theory and Practice (Psi Classics of the Counterinsurgency Era)*. Westport: Praeger, 2006.

Gentile, Gian P. "Let's Build an Army to Win All Wars." *Joint Forces Quarterly* 52, 1st Quarter (2009): 27–33. http://www.thefreelibrary.com/Let's+build+an+army+to+win+all+wars.-a0193510865 (accessed 13 October 2010).

Grau, Lester W. *The Bear Went Over the Mountain: Soviet Combat Tactics in Afghanistan*. Portland: Frank Cass Publishers, 1998.

Gray, Colin S. 2005. *Another Bloody Century: Future Warfare*. London: Phoenix, 2005.

Greenshields, Brian. "Population Control." In *Gangs and Guerrillas: Ideas from Counterinsurgency and Counterterrorism*, edited by Michael Freeman and Hy Rothstein, 77-81. Monterey: Naval Postgraduate School, 2011. http://www.google.com/url?sa= t&rct=j&q=&esrc=s&source=web&cd=1&ved=0CCsQFjAA&url=http%3A%2F%2Fww w.nps.edu%2FAcademics%2FSchools%2FGSOIS%2FDepartments%2FDA%2FDocume nts%2FG%2520%26%2520G%25204_21_2011.pdf&ei=Gd09U4OqBvfesASQ1IHgBQ &usg=AFQjCNF28kuIxYbqUede8t (accessed 5 January 2014).

Joes, Anthony James. *Resisting Rebellion: The History and Politics of Counterinsurgency.* Lexington: University Press of Kentucky, 2006.

Kilcullen, David. *Counterinsurgency.* New York: Oxford University Press, 2010.

_____. *The Accidental Guerrilla: Fighting Small Wars in the Midst of a Big One.* New York: Oxford University Press, 2009.

Krepinevich Jr., Andrew F. *The Army and Vietnam.* Baltimore: Johns Hopkins University Press, 1986.

Landsdale, Edward G. *In the Midst of Wars: An American's Mission to Southeast Asia.* Fordham: Fordham University Press, 1991.

Lawrence, T. E. "27 Articles." *TE Lawrence Studies.* http://www.telstudies.org/writings/ works/articles_essays/1917_twenty-seven_articles.shtml (accessed 21 February 2014).

Lind, Michael. *Vietnam: The Necessary War: A Reinterpretation of America's Most Disastrous Military Conflict.* New York: Simon and Schuster, 1999.

Lujan, Fernando. *Light Footprints: The Future of American Military Intervention.* Voices From the Field. Washington: Center for a New American Security, 2013. http://www.cnas. org/publications/reports/light-footprints-the-future-of-american-military-intervention#.U0mc9-9OXX4 (accessed February 12, 2014).

Manwaring, Max, and Court Prisk, eds. *El Salvador at War: An Oral History of Conflict from the 1979 Insurrection to the Present.* Washington, DC: National Defense University Press, 1988.

McCormick, Gordon. "Seminar in Guerrilla Warfare." Lecture series. Monterey, CA: Naval Postgraduate School, July-September, 2009.

McCormick, Gordon, and Frank Giordano. "Things Come Together: Symbolic Violence and Guerrilla Mobilisation." *Third World Quarterly* 28, no. 2 (2007): 295-332. http://www.tandfonline.com/doi/abs/10.1080/01436590601153705#.U0mxoO9OXX4 (accessed 12 April 2014).

McDougal, Walter A. *Promised Land, Crusader State: The American Encounter with the World Since 1776.* Boston, MA: Mariner Books, 1997.

Montgomery, Tommie Sue. *Revolution in El Salvador: From Civil Strife to Civil Peace.* Boulder, CO: Westview Press, 1995.

Nagl, John A. "Let's Win the Wars We're In." *Joint Forces Quarterly* 52 (1st Quarter 2009): 20–26. http://www.au.af.mil/au/awc/awcgate/jfq/nagl_win_wars.pdf (accessed 13 October 2010).

Nagl, John A., and Peter J. Schoomaker, *Learning to Eat Soup with a Knife: Counterinsurgency Lessons from Malaya and Vietnam* (Chicago: The University of Chicago Press, 2005).

Neuman, Stephanie G. *Military Assistance in Recent Wars: the Dominance of the Superpowers.* Vol. 122. Washington: Praeger Publishers, 1987.

O'Neill, Tip, and William Novak. *Man of the House: The Life and Political Memoirs of Speaker Tip O'Neill.* New York: Random House, 1987.

Palmer, Dave R. *Summons of the Trumpet: U.S.-Vietnam in Perspective.* Novato: Presidio Press, 1995.

Paret, Peter, ed. "Clausewitz," in *Makers of Modern Strategy.* Princeton: Princeton University Press, 1986.

Rail, R. A. *El Salvador Advisor: Toward a Military Personnel Advisory Doctrine.* Kansas City, MO: Ragal Limited Editions, 1992.

Russell, Philip L. *El Salvador in Crisis.* Austin, TX: Colorado River Press, 1984.

Schmidt, Steffen. W. *El Salvador: America's Next Vietnam?* Salisbury, NC: Documentary Publications, 1983.

Schwartz, Benjamin. *American Counterinsurgency Doctrine and El Salvador: The Frustrations of Reform and the Illusions of Nation Building.* Santa Monica: RAND, 1991.

Sepp, Kalev. "Best Practices in Counterinsurgency." *Military Review* (May-June 2005): 8-12. http://www.google.com/url?sa=t&rct=j&q=&esrc=s&source=web&cd=1&ved=0CCYQF jAA&url=http%3A%2F%2Fwww.au.af.mil%2Fau%2Fawc%2Fawcgate%2Fmilreview% 2Fsepp.pdf&ei=H-09U6zcEcutsASZjYCYCg&usg=AFQjCNFjZWHBxdk Acti4gaRFphr4NkL6XQ&bvm=bv.64125504,d.cWc (accessed 29 December 2013).

Shaull, Wendy. *Tortillas, Beans, and M-16s: A Year with the Guerrillas in El Salvador.* London: Pluto Press, 1990.

Sheehan, Neil. A *Bright Shining Lie: John Paul Vann and America in Vietnam.* New York: Random House, 1988.

Spector, Ronald. *Advise and Support: The Early Years, 1941-1960.* Washington, DC: Center For Military History, 1983.

Stanley, William. *The Protection Racket State: Elite Politics, Military Extortion, and Civil War in El Salvador.* Philadelphia, PA: Temple University Press, 1996.

Summers, Harry. *On Strategy: A Critical Analysis of the Vietnam War.* New York: Presidio Press, 1995.

Taylor, Brian, and Roxana Botea, "Tilly Tally: War-Making and State-Making in the Contemporary Third World," *International Studies Review* 10, no. 1 (2008): 27-56, 28-29.

Tilly, Charles. *Coercion, Capital and European States: AD 990-1992*. Cambridge: Blackwell, 1990.

Tse-Tung, Mao. *Mao Tse-Tung On the Protracted War*. Beijing: Foreign Languages Press, 1960.

Trinquier, Roger. *Modern Warfare: a French View of Counterinsurgency*. Translated from the French by Daniel Lee with an introduction by Bernard B. Fall, and foreword by Eliot A. Cohen. Westport, CT: Praeger, 2006.

Tzu, Sun. *The Art of War*. Translated by Samuel B. Griffith. New York: Oxford University Press, 1963.

Van Evera, Stephen. *Guide to Methods for Students of Political Science*. Ithaca: Cornell University Press, 1997.

Waghelstein, John. "Reading the tea leaves: Proto-insurgency in Honduras." *CIWAG Case Study Series 2011-2012*. Edited by Andrea Dew and Marc Genest. Newport, RI: US Naval War College, 2012.

Wilson, Greg. "The Mystic Diamond: Applying the Diamond Model of Counterinsurgency in the Philippines." In *Gangs and Guerrillas: Ideas from Counterinsurgency and Counterterrorism*. Edited by Michael Freeman and Hy Rothstein. Monterey: Naval Postgraduate School, 2011. http://www.google.com/url?sa=t&rct=j&q=&esrc= s&source=web&cd=1&ved=0CCsQFjAA&url=http%3A%2F%2Fwww.nps.edu%2FAca demics%2FSchools%2FGSOIS%2FDepartments%2FDA%2FDocuments%2FG%2520% 26%2520G%25204_21_2011.pdf&ei=Gd09U4OqBvfesASQ1IHgBQ&usg=AFQjCNF28 kuIxYbqUede8t (accessed 5 January 2014).

_____. "Anatomy of a Successful COIN Operation: OEF-Philippines and the Indirect Approach." *Military Review* 86, no. 6 (November-December 2006): 38-48.

Wood, Elisabeth Jean. *Insurgent Collective Action and Civil War in El Salvador*. New York: Cambridge University Press, 2003.

Government Documents

Chairman, Joint Chiefs of Staff. Joint Publication (JP) 3-05, *Special Operations*. Washington, DC: Government Printing Office, 2011. http://www.fas.org/irp/doddir/dod/jp3-05.pdf). (accessed 6 October 2013).

_____. Joint Publication (JP) 5-0, *Joint Operations Planning*. Washington, DC: Government Printing Office, 2011.

_____. Joint Publication (JP) 3-22, *Foreign Internal Defense*. Washington DC: Government Printing Office, 2012.

Department of the Army. Army Doctrine Publication (ADP) 3-0, *Unified Land Operations.* Washington, DC: Government Printing Office, 2011. http://armypubs.army.mil/doctrine/ DR_pubs/dr_a/pdf/adp3_0.pdf (accessed 5 August 2013).

_____. Army Doctrine Publication (ADP) 3-07, *Stability*. Washington, DC: Government Printing Office, 15 February 2013. http://armypubs.army.mil/doctrine/ DR_pubs/dr_a/pdf/adp3_07.pdf) (accessed 5 August 2013).

Department of the Army. Field Manual (FM) 3-24, *Counterinsurgency*. Washington, DC: Government Printing Office, 15 December 2006. https://armypubs.us.army.mil/doctrine/ DR_pubs/dr_a/pdf/fm3_24.pdf) (accessed 8 August 2013).

www.ingramcontent.com/pod-product-compliance
Lightning Source LLC
Chambersburg PA
CBHW080524290526
45790CB00006B/2308